HOW TO TRAIN *Your* DRAGON

CELINE SPARKS

Publishing Designs, Inc.
Huntsville, Alabama

Publishing Designs, Inc.
P.O. Box 3241
Huntsville, Alabama 35810

© 2019 Celine Sparks

Cover illustration: Phyllis Alexander
Book design: CrosslinCreative.net
Images: iStock, VectorStock

Editors: Debra G. Wright, Peggy Coulter

Printed in the United States of America

Publisher's Cataloging-in-Publication Data

Sparks, Celine, 1965—

How to Train Your Dragon / Celine Sparks.

Thirteen chapters.

1. Biblical motivation. 2. The tongue. 3. Humor.

I. Title.

ISBN 978-1-945127-13-7

248.8

DEDICATION

To Scotty, who has seen the worst of my dragon,
and nudged it back on the leash.

ENDORSEMENTS

Celine, you have done it again! Thank you for courageously and humorously tackling that dreadful dragon called the tongue and enabling us to see, not only its danger, but also its ability to soothe, encourage, and uplift any sister in her walk with the Lord.

> —Becky Blackmon, author of *The Begging Place*, *A Pearl Seeker*, and *Seek the Precious Moments*

The gospel is fundamentally a message of joy. Celine uses humor to teach some great truths in ways that are amusing to read, easy to remember, and key to spiritual growth. I recommend it for both personal and group study.

> —Janie Craun, former editor, *Christian Woman* magazine

Celine has been the key leader of the Horizons Players drama group and is an excellent teacher. She loves the Lord and His Word and has a unique ability to communicate in powerful and thought-provoking ways. You will see this very quickly when you start your journey through this book. You will be blessed for reading her efforts. Enjoy the ride!

> —Kirk Brothers, president, Heritage Christian University
> Florence, Alabama

Celine Sparks allows her readers to relate to her, understanding that she has struggles too. This makes her advice even more valuable. *How to Train Your Dragon* helps us go from biting our tongues to bringing them under submission.

> —Brittney Kennedy, student, Tupelo, Mississippi

I have so enjoyed this delightful and meaningful book that points out the importance of training the tongue (aka dragon). Every Christian needs to read this!

> —Roy Johnson, director, Lads to Leaders and Leaderettes

As is her trademark, Celine uses humor to pique and sustain our interest, but she writes very seriously about the effects of an uncontrolled tongue. She reminds us through Scripture that God holds our "dragons" accountable. Each lesson suggests ways to use our tongues more effectively. "Training Points" sections provide opportunities to evaluate and motivate our progress. This sensitive "dragon" subject is presented in a delightful and rewarding way.

—Carol Dodd, retired teacher, Huntsville, Alabama

Celine has such a creative way of presenting God's truth. I laughed, I cried, and I was convicted. How did she know the "dragons" in my life that need training? I was especially challenged by the lesson "Train Your Dragon to Rescue."

—Rosemary McKnight, author of *I Love Me, I Love Me Not* and
Those Who Wait

Celine made me laugh and cry too, while giving me insightful viewpoints that I never heard before on scriptures about the tongue, particularly on Job, his wife, and friends. I will be forever touched by this truthful point. *"No matter what hardship we may encounter, we are in Christ (Romans 6:3) and He is in us (Romans 8:10). You can't get any closer than that."*

—Brenda Johnson, Lads to Leaders and Leaderettes

Great books catch your attention from the first sentence. Really great books inspire you to become a clearer reflection of Christ. Celine's book does both. You are drawn in from the first hilarious story, and as you continue to read you will be challenged to look truthfully at sins that are often excused. Her skillful applications of scriptures help train our "dragons" once and for all.

—Tracie Shannon, first lady, Freed-Hardeman University

CONTENTS

INTRODUCTION

I was in line at a department store. The pitch was getting higher and the volume louder. Everyone turned their heads to see if we needed to dodge in case things actually started being thrown. But it was a dragon war. The worst kind. Because we know what's true of sticks and stones. They leave resilient victims, ready to fight another day.

But James chapter 3 talks about an unruly and untamable beast. I call it the dragon. It leaves invisible wounds, internal scars, and its velocity can crush your spirit before you can duck.

The tongue. The strongest muscle in the body gets plenty of exercise. We can ponder how something so small can wreak havoc of Titanic proportions. We can ponder, but it's nothing James didn't already ponder two thousand years ago (vv. 4–5).

Those of us who care have tried. We've held daily wrestling matches with that dragon, and as sure as we subdue him long enough to turn and unbar the door, he meets us on the other side. It's been lamented throughout history that we can't put back what he spits out. So what do we do?

Well, back to the department store line. The cashier and the customer were in a shout-off. We've heard that the customer is always right, but the cashier wasn't buying it. In fact, none of us were buying anything because the line was at a standstill. We shuffled our feet. We kind of looked down. The tension was thickening, and I'm pretty sure if there was a security camera somewhere, our picture will soon be next to the dictionary entry: Awkward. A spirit of negativity covered the floor. And then it happened.

I don't know her name, but she sure had a way with her dragon. A woman near the front of the line turned toward us, and I moaned under my breath as I knew she was about to throw in her two cents. And I could guess the first penny: *Puh-lease, can we just get someone to wait on us here? The nerve of some people who think they can push everyone else around. This is ridiculous.* But her dragon didn't say any of those things. Her dragon said in a healthy volume, "Has anyone been to the butterfly display at the botanical gardens?"

Smiles started popping up like election signs in November.

I was the first to answer, "I have."

The others followed quickly.

"Oh, it's beautiful. We went at peak season."

"Oh, I know, and we got the best pictures."

"One landed on my toddler's nose, and he screamed like it was a wasp."

How did this woman do that? She took one of the most negative moments I have experienced while shopping and turned it into one of the most positive ones.

That's the only way we can successfully deal with our dragon. James has already told us we can't tame it. The only logical answer is to keep it distracted with good and positive things. That dragon can be more useful than we imagine if we don't give him time to resort back to his nature.

Butterflies. What, in this wide world of creation, could possibly be more positive or beautiful than butterflies? Not much. But then again, there are some things. Evangelism. Prayer. Encouragement. Teaching. Laughter.

That's the focus of this book. Beautiful things, commands of God that dispel the negative potential of the tongue. Join with me in a study not so much of how to tame the dragon, but how to better it, how to train it. Laugh with me, learn with me, turn pages of your worn Bible with me, and mark them up if it helps. But hold on to your dragon; it's going to be a wild ride!

Celine

The Dragon
UNLEASHED
Curse God and Die

Key Scriptures
Job 1; Job 2:10; James 3

Lassie, the Flower-Power Dog

Leashes don't work very well for animals that aren't used to them. We had a mangy dog when we were growing up; she was my best friend. Apparently, we weren't nearly as good with original names when it came to pets as my mom was when it came to naming me. (Let's not even talk about my middle name.) We named the collie *Lassie*.

Lassie never attended obedience school, so "A child left to himself brings shame to his mother" (Proverbs 29:15) applied to our situation in every way. Lassie pretty much did what she wanted to do. When she decided to walk a mile to my school and into the sixth-grade classroom and down the row to the desk where I sat mortified as the teacher was crying, "Shoo! Shoo!" she didn't ask permission. When she wanted to lie on her back in a newly dug ditch after a good rain, and do the neutron dance, no one stopped her. If

she wanted to bark the entirety of *War and Peace* at 3:00 AM for no reason, she didn't ask anyone first. She was the poster child for the sixties. At a time when it was advocated to do your own thing and let it all hang out, she obliged.

No Leader for Lassie

To add to Lassie's lack of training, we didn't even own a leash, so when the rabies clinic came to our neighborhood, my mom created a makeshift one with nylon rope. As if this wasn't embarrassing enough, when my mother gave a slight tug on the "leash" to summon the dog out of the car, she refused. The same thing happened with the following yank, hoist, heave, and family game of grunt and pull. Lassie was not budging no matter how sweetly we called her name, pled with her, bribed and threatened. Mom finally resorted to picking her up, greasy mange treatment and all, stumbling to the veterinary table with her, plopping her down and saying, "There!"

That was the day that we were pretty much done with leashes. We should have given it one more chance. Later on, we were going to the cabin at the river for the weekend, and we begged to bring her along. It would have worked fine if our car had not had an engine failure in downtown Birmingham. My dad tinkered with it as long as he could in the traffic before calling a cab. We all unloaded out of the station wagon with our fishing poles and tackle boxes to board the taxi—all of us but one. Lassie again had a standoff, except this time, when my mom lifted her, I guess the mange treatment was greasy enough for Lassie to slip through her arms. And she was off, running down the sidewalks of downtown Birmingham, my dad weaving through the shoppers chasing her within a block of where he held a dignified job Monday through Friday. I'm glad he didn't carry a gun.

Tongue on a Leash

In both instances, if Lassie had been trained to use a leash, all of the complete chaos would have been avoided. Is there a lesson for us here? How much trouble and utter devastation could be avoided if we could just learn to keep our tongues on a leash, if we could just control what slips through our lips like a greased dog?

We tend to excuse ourselves and think that leashes are great when our days are a cake walk in the park, but on rabies-shot days and high traffic/car breakdown days, it's somehow okay for our tongues to unleash.

Some days are like that. Some days the weather won't cooperate, the check bounces, the moth balls didn't work, and you're afraid to ask what's in the playpen. It's those times that our tongues break off from their leashes and tear into the nearest innocent bystander. In that setting, we're really not responsible for anything that comes out of our mouths. Or are we?

Morals and Money—What a Catch!

Flash back for a moment to a prominent woman in history. She was on top of the world. Her pearls were real, and her fur was long. When she walked arm in arm with her husband, the community watched, and talked.

I don't have scripture to specifically back those claims, but I imagine that's the way it was, because I do have one scripture that says it all, "This man was the greatest of all the people of the east" (Job 1:3). This verse follows a description of Job's material wealth.

What first lady ever had it as good as Mrs. Job? What world leader, movie star, or investment-firm leader ever laid that claim? But it gets so much better. Not only was her man a millionaire (in our vernacular), but he was also a good man. In fact, he was the best. Not only did he lavishly bestow his wife with earthly treasures, but his integrity was so outstanding that scripture tells us "that man was blameless and upright, and one who feared God and turned away from evil" (Job 1:1).

What a catch! It was as near a perfect world as we can get this side of heaven, because in addition

What first lady ever had it as good as Mrs. Job?

to the marriage and the possessions, they had a great family life—seven sons and three daughters. Job was all about being a father. Every day, Job was concerned—not just about what those children were doing religiously on the outside, but even the thoughts they were thinking on the inside (Job 1:5). Wouldn't you like to have this guy conduct a parenting seminar at your congregation?

He would rise early in the morning and offer burnt offerings according to the number of them all. For Job said, "It may be that my sons have sinned and cursed God in their hearts." Thus Job did regularly (Job 1:5).

For Better—or for Worse

Everything was right in Mrs. Job's world . . . until that day. She knew something was wrong as soon as Job walked through the door of that huge mansion. Job's hair was gone—shaven. His robe was torn. Something was very wrong. Something bad. Her heart sank immediately into her stomach; she was nauseated, chilled, and weak in the knees. Where was her confident man of leadership? She was afraid to ask.

When Mrs. Job learned that all of their assets were gone in one instant, with no warning, I imagine it was a devastating blow. There had been a tornado, there had been a fire, there had been several raids—all in the same day. How do you go from riches to rags in one day? She was about to find out. Still in a state of shock, it would take time for reality to set in.

Behold, a great wind came across the wilderness and struck the four corners of the house, and it fell upon the young people, and they are dead (Job 1:19).

Grief Unleashed Her Tongue

Material wealth is just stuff, and Job, being the spiritual giant that he was, had to know that. They would recover together. But the next news was unthinkable. The babies Mrs. Job had carried and nursed at her breasts, rocked and walked, taught and nourished, cradled, played with, bandaged, laughed with, had late night talks with drying their tears, guided them on the path to adulthood—all of her precious sons and daughters were gone. "Honey, they're dead. They're not coming back," I can hear Job wailing.

Then I imagine she began to name names, all of the names of her children. Screaming at times, barely whispering at others. Questioning. Walking in circles. Dazed. Banging her head against the wall, repeating "No," and praying somehow it wasn't true.

That's the scene I imagine. The Bible never even tells us how she received the news or what she did next. But being a mother, I can't imagine it any differently. I know the God who had a conversation with Satan about Job, who put those babies in Mrs. Job's womb, who promised He'd never leave us or forsake us, who watched as His own Son bled and died in a brutal scene—I know that He was there with her, as He has been with every one of His children who has ever been pained with the death of a child.

As valuable as that assurance is, it doesn't change the circumstances of the grief, and grief sometimes calls out in the irrational tones of a confused and broken language.

I believe that's what it did within Mrs. Job.

Then his wife said to him, "Do you still hold fast your integrity? Curse God and die!" (Job 2:9).

Grief had run amuck, but it had not run its gamut until now. Watching her husband, once the most esteemed man in the hemisphere, now in poverty and misery, scraping oozing sores with a broken piece of a flower pot, she spoke what should never be uttered.

Vile Words from Treasured Lips

Job's response was remarkable. How can you keep your chin up when your soulmate has turned on you—the one whose intimacy with you produced ten children, who shared with you your greatest burden when you broke the heartwrenching news? How many times had she cried on his shoulder? How many times had they stayed awake hurting together? Before the tide turned, how many times had they prayed together, reasoned together, dreamed of what each unique child could one day become in God's service? Remember, Job was the kind of man who prayed with and about his family. How many times had he laughed with her when she tripped on the furniture? How often had she stroked his hair when she wondered what was behind those pensive eyes?

And now it had come to this—the vilest stream spilling from what had once been the most treasured lips. Was Job now past the point of shock? Did his own voice quiver as he mustered the words, "You speak as one of the foolish women"?

Not only had her own tongue jumped off the leash, but she was also standing like a cow in the road, blocking his view of any hope that was ahead, giving him the ultimatum of a U-turn or a head-on collision.

Can we blame her? Certainly! It's never okay to blaspheme God. It's never okay to tell a loved one to "just die, all right?" But if ever there were circumstances that would warrant one to "speak as one of the foolish women," and there aren't, it would be Mrs. Job's.

 But he said to her, "You speak as one of the foolish women would speak. Shall we receive good from God, and shall we not receive evil?" In all this Job did not sin with his lips (Job 2:10).

Are We Foolish Women?

Now what was our excuse again? A bad day at work? A bad day at home? Lost keys, lost paycheck, lost job, dent in the fender, three kids with the stomach bug? Whatever it is, and there are truly some great trials I've seen loved ones suffer through, it might make a pretty high stack of agony, but I'm thinking Mrs. Job's stack might edge it out just a hair.

When we've had a bad day, does it give our tongues the right to jump off the leash, or even to stand out in the middle of the road, blocking others from a good view of God? Job said that's when we speak as one of the foolish women.

Maybe we haven't told our loved ones to curse God and die, but from our speech alone, would we be regarded as one of the foolish women? Just who are these women Job referred to? I don't know, but in Old Testament writing, the word *foolish* is almost always an allusion to idol seekers—those who do not trust in the living God.

 But no human being can tame the tongue. It is a restless evil, full of deadly poison (James 3:8).

Tame It or Train It?

Before you and I jump to a denial of that, we probably should check the leash. It's interesting that James, living in times we think of as primitive—walking around with a camel who had never even seen an ice cream sandwich, much less a touch screen that tells you what to do next—said that every animal and beast of the sea had been tamed (James 3:7). What? This was before Barnum and Bailey and before Sea World. We're talking about whales, elephants, and poisonous snakes. Apparently, Shamu and Dumbo arrived late on the scene. And there are references to snake charming in Psalm 58:4–5 and in Jeremiah 8:17.

But there was that one beast; James did make an exception to it. There is that one villain that, like in the sci-fi movies, you can't whip, beat, hypnotize, shoot, or strangle. Only it's not a sci-fi creature. It's real, and it's lying there in your mouth right now.

That beast is the untamable dragon. It's just a little thing, but it boasts with the biggest of them (James 3:5). And just like those dragons of medieval lore, it's a fire-breathing one. "How great a forest is set ablaze by such a small fire! And the tongue is a fire, a world of unrighteousness.

The tongue is set among our members, staining the whole body, setting on fire the entire course of life, and set on fire by hell" (James 3:5–6). Move over, Godzilla! There's not a horror movie in Hollywood that can claim to compare to the dragon-tongue described here. But these films are fiction; Hollywood's dragons only cause nightmares in your sleep. God's Word is truth; the beast it talks about is real, and it can cause nightmares when we're awake.

So what do we do? James has already said we can't tame it, so we've got to train it. We've got to subdue it, control it, keep it on a leash.

But it's not always about what the tongue is not doing. We've got to train the creature to fill its time with positive things for the kingdom, so there will be less propensity to break off the chain at any given time.

Life is a circus. Our dragons are in the ring. We've got to check the chain and strengthen the links. Let's go!

> With it we bless our Lord and Father, and with it we curse people who are made in the likeness of God. From the same mouth come blessing and cursing. My brothers, these things ought not to be so (James 3:9–10).

TRAINING POINTS

1. Leash laws are a relatively new addition to society. Share a true anecdote about an aggressive animal off its leash. How do these episodes parallel our tongue in the danger or chaos that ensued?

2. How many *whys* did Job express in chapter 3 of his book? Do you think these are a contrast to his initial response to tragedy in chapter 1? Do you think the time spent in questioning was healthy and necessary to the grieving process?

3. What, to you, was the lowest moment in the story of Job?

4. We have all seen—maybe been a part of—families who went from
   life-as-usual to tragedy in an instant. How does a Christian family or
   individual anchor in times like those, and how does it differ, if at all,
   from those outside of Christ?

5. Do we ever excuse our tongues because of circumstances? Is it warranted? On the flip side, are there times we should be more patient
   with other people's tongues, even those of our sisters? If so, list some
   examples.

6. Because the book of Job ends well for him and his family, I like to
   think his wife's "unleashed" moment was one she wished she could
   take back. We all know we can't take back what has escaped the cage.
   However, what are some steps we can take in an effort to somehow
   minimize and reverse the damage?

7. Write a note this week to a mother who has lost a child. It may have
   been years ago. It may have been a miscarriage or a mature adult.
   You may have lost one yourself and understand the power of the relationship that never fades. Just drop a few encouraging words remembering the beauty of that life and communicating the love you have
   for the mother.

8. Mrs. Job had ten children. What do you think of the idea that whether
   ten or only one or two, the grief would have been the same because
   every child holds the whole of your heart? Do you agree or disagree?
   Why?

9. Lassie's makeshift leash did not work. What things do we incorporate
   in our lives to keep our tongues leashed? Do we ever substitute makeshift leashes when we get too busy for these? How does that work out?

10. When catastrophe strikes, how does our first reaction differ from our "collected" reaction? Think of a specific example from your experiences. It's impossible to prepare our tongues for the bombs that drop in our lives unforeseen. Or is it? If there is a way to keep our minds on guard to grab the tongue's leash, share it.

THE TAIL END

And Speaking of Car Breakdown, Leashes, Birmingham, and the Circus . . .

It's hard to accept, but we knew it was coming. All earthly relationships have an expiration date. We had been down many roads together, but she was beginning to choke at the smallest things, she would blow a fuse over nothing at all, and to tell you the truth, I think her universal joint was falling out.

We had hoped to hold onto our family SUV a few years longer. We had three children in college at the same time, and we'd stretched the ends so much already to make them meet that they looked like the neck hole on a T-shirt borrowed from Godzilla. So if we could have just duct taped the vehicle together until graduation of the next year, picking up a car payment would have been a little more doable by then.

But our car didn't come with a factory-installed sense of timing. In fact, we were planning to leave the next Monday to visit that same college where all our money was, so we could wave to it from a little closer proximity. And Friday, I was supposed to fly to Dallas. But this was Thursday, so just like the rest of us, the car waited until the last minute to do something important—tell us she couldn't make the trip on Monday.

I backed out of the driveway for an errand, and when I put her in gear to go forward, she was a little hesitant. In fact, she behaved exactly the way my son did the first day of kindergarten. I smiled, nudged, pushed, pulled, demanded, and offered a dozen frosted cookies, but the car wasn't budging.

My husband and I spent the next four hours online looking for a model we could afford.

"Hey, here's a nice little model with just a moderate amount of storm damage."

"Moderate? The front windshield is out and the passenger door is hanging on the back bumper!"

"Well, the price is right. Hey, how about this? Red sedan; 89K miles; one owner."

"Look at the interior! Who was the one owner, Edward Scissorhands?"

But eventually we found ourselves doing what all responsible adults have to do at some stage of their life, walk around in a parking lot under an enormous inflated gorilla and meander through balloons tied to every luggage rack.

An hour later, we were sitting at the desk of a used car salesman making small talk about the weather, taco recipes, and our pets back home, but all of this was a cover for the actual conversation that was going on under the table as my husband and I passed the phone back and forth with new texts.

"Offer him 9500."

"What if he counters?"

And then to the sales manager . . .

"Yep, counters are perfect for placing all the taco toppings."

"Counter back."

"Should I ask if he'll guarantee the 2.5 financing?"

"Yes, but don't come across cocky."

"Our cocker spaniel loves the Spanish olives."

"If the payment is over 325, we'll have to disconnect the heat on the first floor of the house."

"But if we don't get a car by tomorrow, we'll have to walk to the college."

"Walk? Yeah, we walk her every night. We've got a long leash."

"A long lease would get the payments down even more."

"Yeah, but when the lease is up?"

"Ask if he can do financing for 60 months a bit lower than 48."

"It was lower than 48 last night, but it's supposed to warm up after the rain."

And speaking of rain, it just sprinkled the day we looked at the car until they told us to go move the contents of our former car into the new one. And then there was a torrential downpour. And I had worn suede shoes. Try moving two cases of new paperback books in sock feet holding a blanket over the boxes so there's no damage. Was it coincidence that as we were pulling out of the parking lot, the radio announced that the circus, after a 146-year run, had just come to an end?

But we were out of there with a new set of wheels. The whole car-buying experience took me back a few years to my dad's part-time business, Holder & Son Motors. He didn't have a car lot with an inflated gorilla. But when he came home from his regular job at the telephone company, he did a little car trading.

Occasionally the extra cash would time out just right for a new pair of gym shoes or a week of camp, but the turnover of cars we drove did not time out right at all. This is illustrated by the fact that I was 16 and driving an asparagus colored AMC Hornet to high school. A Hornet! Who has even heard of a Hornet outside of the kind that sting cattlemen in Western movies? Now I was driving one, and the embarrassment was heightened by the fact that my dad had put our home phone number in a large font on the back windshield with white shoe polish. What was he thinking?

But he advertised however he could. He couldn't afford a big billboard so he successfully placed little ads in the classifieds. In a town the size of Birmingham, his little ad competed against thousands of others. What were the chances that at a pep rally where shredded newspaper confetti was all over the gym, a boy would pick up a piece of it, hand it to my sister with the line, "Wanna buy a used car?" and somehow that would have her phone number on it? The odds are better than you think.

After scores of strangers coming to our driveway before the days of Craig's List, evenings spent driving to grocery store lots to park the cars in conspicuous spaces we had rented, and many a disappointed moment when I ran to the phone hoping it was the guy in chemistry class only to hear, "How many miles does the Vega have?" the business finally folded.

Dad moved to a place in the country and preferred planting trees to writing bills of sale. I can no longer check his inventory when I find myself in the recent predicament of needing a replacement right away. But at any rate, we have a new ride. She will last a few years, and then her crank shaft will get a little too cranky or a little too shafty, or her exhaust pipe will get a little too exhausted. We'll haul in, sputter down the road, and do a little more horse trading. I'm not sure what shenanigans will befall us this time, but I fully expect to hear on the radio as we pull out of the lot . . .

"We have reports that the circus has just made a comeback."

No friend is more valued than he who keeps his mouth shut at just the right time.

—Celine Sparks

Train Your Dragon to SIT

Be Silent

Key Scriptures
Job 13; James 5:7–11;
Job 40:4; James 1:19

"Sit!" It seems like the simplest of tricks to teach an animal. It is not. Sometimes if you tell a dog to sit, he will do it. This is because you gently put pressure on his back end with the heel of your shoe. This has never worked for any of our dogs. They just seem to say, "A little lower . . . Ahh, that's good right there. Now scratch a little harder. No, don't stop."

No, dogs never sit when you tell them to. They wait until you take them to the park in front of people, and you throw random objects and say, "Fetch!" They have command confusion disorder, CCD, which can spread rapidly from the dog to the children. This is where the dog thinks that "fetch" means "sit," and so the more you try to coerce the dog into fetching, the more he is convinced beyond any reasonable doubt that he should firmly sit.

It's worse with cats.

That dragon in your mouth isn't too good at "sit" either.

"Voluntary" Requires Thought

I'm thankful for the many involuntary organs we have in our bodies—the heart, the lungs, the kidneys. These work without our ever giving a thought to them. The tongue should not be one of those organs. Unfortunately, for some of us, it often is.

We usually manage pretty well when our dragons stay in their lair, asleep. Job's friends showed up with their dragons resting, and for all the things Bildad, Zophar, and Eliphaz did wrong, they did a few things right.

> Now when Job's three friends heard of all this adversity that had come upon him, each one came from his own place—Eliphaz the Temanite, Bildad the Shuhite, and Zophar the Naamathite. For they had made an appointment together to come and mourn with him, and to comfort him (Job 2:11 NKJV).

- *They cared enough to travel apparently great distances just to be with Job.* They are called his friends, and what a glimpse of hope it must have been, after his wife had kicked him when he was down and then twisted the heel for emphasis, to now see familiar outlines appearing on the horizon. Second only to the voice in recognition is a person's walk. Friend, farmer, and philosopher Charlie Coats once told me, "No two fellers walk the same."

  So there they were, friends in the time of despair, distinctively differing from one another in their strides. They didn't change anything. They couldn't undo tornadoes or poverty or tragic massacres. But they could be there. And at times when there is nothing else to be done, being there resonates a love and care unspoken by the dragon.

- *This wasn't a casual chance meeting, but a collaborated effort, circled on the calendar.* It probably wasn't going to happen, considering the distance between the three—"each came from his own place"—and the separate but usual demands of life, except that they made it happen. Good intentions often get buried in business as usual, and opportunities expire like cereal coupons you meant to use. All the more remarkable is the fact that this little committee coordinated this with no texts, emails, or private messages at their fingertips or in their hip pockets.

To have such a miserable end, they couldn't have had a better start. Though they didn't recognize him because his rags had erased any resemblance to his riches, he surely recognized them as they cried out in tears (Job 2:12). They sat with him on the ground for seven days. That's friendship. That's being with him. They weren't sitting in lavish funeral home chairs, but on the ground. Seven days.

I bet you have friends like Job's. In times of crisis, they'll make a cot out of two chairs in a hospital room, and they won't remember they even have hair to wash for days on end if need be. They are Bildad, Eliphaz, and Zophar in the "before" pictures.

And they sat with him on the ground seven days and seven nights, and no one spoke a word to him, for they saw that his suffering was very great (Job 2:13).

Unleashed Dragons Won't Sit

Before the dragons were unleashed, Job's dragon played the first card. "After this, Job opened his mouth and cursed the day of his birth" (3:1). Beginning in chapter 4, Job's know-it-all friends begin to accuse him falsely with no basis, and to give unsolicited advice. They continue to ramble on for the greater part of a moderately lengthy book, and at times it would be humorous, if not so serious. "Miserable comforters are you all," Job said (16:2). God was not amused (42:7). Throughout the discourse, Job demands to speak to God. In a paraphrased synopsis, Job says, "I want some answers!" and God says, "You don't even know all the questions yet."

How often do our dragons mimic Bildad, Eliphaz, Zophar, and even Job when they were doing much better sitting, resting, and trusting? Their unleashed tongues didn't even fit the descriptions of what we usually teach against. They weren't cursing and telling dirty jokes or whopper lies—at least not intentionally. In fact, it was an intensely religious discourse in its orientation. But it was wrong. Sit down, tongues! You don't always have to have the answer for why a wayward child turned that way. You don't have to have the formula for the friend whose parents are divorcing. You just have to be there.

Hand over Mouth—and Fingertips

If I lined ten people up and asked them the theme of Job, nine-and-a-half of them would say patience. It's a good answer, and one you find in scripture itself (James 5:11 KJV). But there's more. It's not the kind of patience we crave when we encounter long shopping lines and toddlers who get the same question stuck on their tongues for the better part of a day. It's the kind that pulled Job through. Most translations render it *perseverance*—patience on steroids.

And while the lesson for us, from the outside looking in, is perseverance, there was another one for Job. He quipped it himself in this passage:

"Behold, I am of small account; what shall I answer you? I lay my hand on my mouth" (Job 40:4).

It's one way to keep from saying something when you shouldn't. We do it to small children all the time. We find that our children have extraordinarily big mouths for the size of their bodies, so that when a stranger walks by with a noticeable hat and walking a Doberman in a tutu, your kid who suddenly thinks you must be hard of hearing, says, "Whoa! Look at ———!" That triggers your hand to automatic mode, and before he can get another syllable out, he finds the palm of your hand resting gently over every opening of his face.

Oh, that we could silence our own lips as quickly as we can those of our children. How much better our days would be if we could be like Job, realize that we don't have the answer, and put our hands over our mouths!

James says it best, because the Word of God always does:

> Let every person be quick to hear, slow to speak, slow to anger (James 1:19).

Your mama told you just like mine told me: "Two ears; one mouth." We usually get the ratio of activity backward.

Humorist Dave Barry once called the condition Blitherer's Disease. It occurs when every thought that comes into the mind automatically plops out of the mouth (Barry).

I believe, in fact, that when it comes to social media, there has been a bypass, and the route goes directly to the fingertips now. Where is the filter? Where is that hesitation that James recommends: Be slow to speak?

Broken Filters

Filters are great innovations. We put them on the faucet before we'll drink the water. We want a fresh one on the air conditioner vent so we won't breathe the wrong thing. We won't even make a cup of coffee without a filter. How is it that we're perfectly okay with letting every thought escape our mouth without filtering out what would hurt others, what would not honor God, and what would create an atmosphere of criticism and negativity?

A few summers back, we packed up some important things like Cheetos and swim rings, and headed to Pie-Daddy's, the kids' beloved grandfather—the one with the pool. We answered "are we almost there?" until we almost weren't. We pulled into the driveway, and the kids jumped out forgetting to shut the car doors. They had but one thought— a backward cannonball off the diving board. But they stopped just short of it. The deep blue pool they had envisioned for the past two hours was green and icky. No one wanted to swim in that.

Of course the problem was that the

Oh, that we could silence our own lips as quickly as we can those of our children filter was broken. Without constant maintenance, it can happen. Is my filter broken? Without constant maintenance, I can let thoughts escape into the atmosphere without checking them. Unfiltered speech is green and icky. No one wants to swim in that.

Some people boast around, swinging their hips with each slinging of their lips. "Yeah, I said it!"; "I guess I told her!"; "She got an earful!"; and "I call it like I see it." Yeah, you said it! But did you have to?

Remove Your Sound

Consider Job's friends again. They were going to say it or bust. I guess they told him, but told him what? He definitely got an earful, but none of it was helpful or encouraging. And just like all of those who call it like they see it, their vision was off. They were venturing into territory they knew nothing about as if they had personally blazed the trail, staked out the land, and put it on Google Maps.

As children, we were not allowed to say "shut up" to one another, so often one of us would stare down the other, and say, "Remove your sound." Job told his friends,

> Oh that you would keep silent, and it would be your wisdom! (Job 13:5).

If you back up a few verses, you find what kind of language is better left unsaid—telling someone who's discouraged something he already knows; assuming superiority in your words, and making things up that are at best speculation—Job called them lies. These are the ingredients for the "worthless physicians." But the ingredients list for wisdom is shorter: silence.

Remove your sound. Train your dragon to sit.

> Whoever belittles his neighbor lacks sense, but a man of understanding remains silent (Proverbs 11:12).

TRAINING
POINTS

1. Think about a specific person you would listen to if you were in trouble or discouraged. Why? What is it about that person's disposition or lifestyle that makes you want to hear her spiel?

2. Read Job chapters 4, 8, and 11. Examine the speech of each of the three friends. Obviously, they were wrong in their diagnosis and condemnation, yet does each have a personality strength that distinguishes him from the other two? Which personality reminds you the most of your own? How could each strength have been a match for encouragement rather than discouragement?

3. Does social media have more negatives than positives, or vice versa? What kind of posts are a good use of our time and influence? What kind should be avoided and why?

4. List some Bible examples of people who spoke before they thought it through, other than those in the book of Job.

5. What do you think of the philosophy that prefers plain-spoken people because "at least you know where you stand"? Are there times we can be too kind with our language? How so?

— Luke 6:36-37 —

THE TAIL END

And Speaking of Coffee and Shoes . . .

We wear them all winter in the south. A friend gave me a pair of socks divided between the big toe and the "index toe" so that even on really cold days, I could do flip-flops. But as spring approaches, the flip-flop frenzy heightens. We need more to get the same fix, so we have neons and earth tones, sequined ones and striped ones, calico for our spring luncheon and no-nonsense navy flips for the upscale business suit.

We define ourselves not by the factory extras on our cars, but by the frivolity of our flops. And there's something that sounds a little wrong with that—that our idea of success is something that has the actual word "flop" in its name.

But fashion demands more fashion so that when we select the perfect flip-flops from our wall-of-shame shoe racks, we sigh in despair at our underdressed toe nails. There's an app for that. It's called a pedicure, and while I'm not sure it really cures much of anything except our shot at college tuition, there are beautiful posters in the windows of the salon picturing glistening coral and chartreuse toenails in the sand, and we bite. Wait—bad choice of words. These are toenails, so we don't bite, but we do give in to the advertiser.

What are we thinking? These are toenails, people. We could have a tank of gas. We could go to the movies. We could buy *two* cups of outrageous coffee instead of one. We are paying exorbitant amounts of cash with a tip on top of that for toenails. Toenails!

I did it once. I was surrounded by people who weren't even nervous that someone else was handling their feet and that the chair was vibrating underneath them. At these prices, I guess you get it all since the older lady beside me handed the pedicure specialist her tablet and said, "Here! Beat this level of Candy Crush for me." And she did.

But yeah. It was nice. I joined the ranks of those who actually slide their feet out of line a little in the grocery store afterward, imagining that people around them are quoting Song of Solomon 7:1 in their heads, "How beautiful are your feet in sandals, O prince's daughter." It's not quite that way for my husband who alludes to the other beautiful-feet verse concerning those who bring good news, and says, "A 32-dollar debit swipe for this is *not* good news."

Where there's money to be made, be assured, home parties will get their toes in the door too. It seems a little odd to me. At these events, people used to pass plastic bowls around to admire, or sometimes jewelry. But now we're saying, "Pass the toenails."

Oh, toenail decorating parties are not a new thing I guess. What seven-year-old did not shut the bathroom door once with all of her friends and raid the medicine cabinet for toenail polish? It always ended in our being pretty sure there was a death in there, but we're not clear whether the conclusion came from the formaldehyde smell or the bright red splotches on the sink and tile.

But these new parties skip the mess and go straight for the wallet. In fact, often the hostesses have decided to avoid all the stress of houseguests and just request your payment online. They call that a party. What? In addition to being guilt-tripped into supporting your friend's venture, now you've got to do it without even getting any free cheeseball and punch in the deal? And how can you have door prizes if there is no door? What you do get is a set of finger (or toe) nails. And somehow, it just seems a little too ironic for a company that is aimed at beautifying toes to have jam as part of its name. Hmm. Toe. Jam. Toe. Jam. Did no one make the connection? Was everyone just completely exhausted at that executive meeting or what?

These new parties skip the mess and go straight for the wallet.

Anyway, the product is great because it involves wraps in addition to polish, so that instead of just having exotic colors like raspberry petunia, you can also have plaids, paisleys, polka-dots, and unicorns. I guess they're called wraps because the word *stickers* was already taken. No matter what they're called, we'll pay fifteen dollars for the gluten-free vegan wraps, just in case there's a biter, I guess.

See, whatever it takes to get our nails to be noticed, we'll do it. Even our cats are getting in on the act. A few years back, there was one of those "if you order now, you'll get two for the low price of $19.95" commercials. After all, it doesn't really matter how much inflation affects our economy, we will still always be able to buy completely useless things for $19.95. In fact, this particular commercial was for a cat emery board. Are cats asking for this? Is there a huge trend of kitties sitting around gossiping and doing one another's nails? Add to this that the commercial then said the emery board is laced with catnip. What kind of party is this?

I think I'll stick with the online option for human nails. It says they last for six weeks. On my fingernails, that means six weeks of not being able to type, button my shirt, change the channel, or peel the sticker off a banana.

Face it, girls, we've taken vanity to a new level. But don't think that I'm opposed. There are perfectly good reasons to paint, trim, buff, and wallpaper your fingernails and toenails. For instance, you never know when you might happen on a game of hokey-pokey, and with no prior warning at all, you suddenly have to put your left foot in, and shake it all about.

Save embarrassment.

Be prepared.

(Originally printed in *Christian Woman* magazine, M/J 2017)

Train Your Dragon to ROLL OVER

Repent Out Loud

Key Scriptures
Exodus 32; 1 John 1; Romans 3:23;
James 5:16; Proverbs 16:18

"Is that it? You're telling me you paid for a six-week course and this is what your dog can do? By now I'm thinking he should be able to vacuum the den or at least fold a washcloth." That's what I feel like saying when I see a demonstration of what a dog has learned in school. Have we changed the definition of school? Isn't he supposed to be learning letters or numbers or at least colors? Really? Sit and roll over? I've done that much each morning before I even go to the bathroom.

Apparently, rolling over is a really difficult task for a pet, especially when the master wants him to do it. You don't have to think too hard to realize there's a spiritual parallel. Unrepentant dragons won't budge. God called the condition stiff-necked time and again in the Old Testament. Whether because of pleasure, stubbornness, or pride, we refuse to do an about face to turn away from our sin. Our necks won't turn and we won't roll over, although the Master has given His all to make it happen.

Necks Not Turning

In Exodus 32, God was in the very process of making provision for His children spiritually. He was giving Moses the hand-engraved (Exodus 31:18) instructions for their success based on their obedience and reliance on these words. He had already delivered this nation powerfully and mercifully from slavery and oppression, and in unbelievable defiance of His goodness, they were dancing and shouting around a golden calf. How ludicrous!

God obviously knew—He always does—that Moses was about to go to bat for these people, so He gave His own character witness before Moses could attempt to intervene. "I have seen this people, and behold, it is a stiff-necked people" (Exodus 32:9). Because of this, God was ready to destroy the nation, but just five verses later, "the Lord repented of the evil which he thought to do unto his people" (32:14 KJV).

God's heart was moved, but man's neck wasn't. The sin was of in-your-face caliber. Its blatancy and intent was unquestionable. They had formed a false god, an idol. They not only weren't feeling guilty about it; they were celebratory. They were so rowdy with the racket they were making, at first Joshua thought a war had broken out (Exodus 32:17). But the truth was, "the people sat down to eat and drink and rose up to play" (32:6), and they weren't playing Monopoly, and it appeared they weren't too keen on Sorry either.

> They have turned aside quickly out of the way that I commanded them. They have made for themselves a golden calf and have worshiped it and sacrificed to it and said, "These are your gods, O Israel, who brought you up out of the land of Egypt!" (Exodus 32:8).

That's the problem with our dragons. Why can't they simply say, "I'm sorry"? First John 1 tells us why. Our dragons get pretty busy denying the whole problem.

Denial 1: "I've Got This!"

The first kind of denial comes in 1 John 1:6: "If we say we have fellowship with him while we walk in darkness, we lie and do not practice the truth." Sometimes there is a tendency to think if we are all Christians, we have an unwritten understanding with one another that "it's all good." I know you may be a little lax here and I'm way off the path there, but since we all share the claim and the name, we've got a season pass. We can check in and check out with no penalties. Our lives can be near shambles spiritually, and our dragon keeps saying, "I've got this." John says in this verse that it's a lie.

I think it was pretty easy for the Israelites to fall victim to the same rhetoric. They were the people of God, and when the people of God begin to overlook sin with its warning signs because, after all, we're keeping it in here, all in the family, you suddenly have a situation. You suddenly have a very dark hallway full of lost people, all of them saying they're walking in light. Approval gives way to more sin until pretty soon you have a gold cow sitting in your campsite.

This happens when Christians post how very thankful they are for their faith and how that Christ is the most important person in their lives, and this post comes directly from an event where they are asked to compromise priorities for the sake of popularity, status, or reward. The event may cause them to miss worship, give the nod to popular but anti-biblical philosophies, or wear clothes that are way too revealing if we're honest about it. But wait—the whole idea is that we're *not* honest about it. We compensate for the darkness by saying it's light. To feel better about giving in to pressure, our dragons spout off about our faith. I'm not saying it's hypocritical because I think as Christians, Satan's favorite target, we are often deceived. I'm just saying what John's saying: We do not practice the truth.

And I said to them, "Whoever has any gold, let them break it off." So they gave it to me, and I cast it into the fire, and this calf came out (Exodus 32:24).

Denial 2: "It Wasn't Me!"

The denial elevates in 1 John 1:8: "If we say we have no sin, we deceive ourselves, and the truth is not in us." While the first denial photoshops the picture for the sake of the landscape, the second one tries to hurdle obvious obstacles. The dragon lashes out, "It wasn't me"; "This isn't my fault"; "You're the one who . . . "; and "Why is everyone against me?" Aaron was quick to excuse himself by saying, "You know the people, that they are set on evil" (Exodus 32:22). He went so far as to explain that it just kind of happened on its own: People threw their earrings in the fire and a cow walked out. It's one of the most laughable whoppers in all of scripture. While we try to convince others of our innocence, we have instead succeeded in deceiving ourselves. God's summary of Israel's sin in Exodus 32:7 was that they had corrupted themselves. *Mission Impossible* tapes aren't the only things that make a lot of noise before they self-destruct.

Denial 3: "I Haven't Sinned!"

But one more stage of denial comes out in John's teaching. "If we say we have not sinned, we make him a liar, and his word is not in us" (1 John 1:10). How is this different from verse 8? The lie of verse 8 is that we have no sin and of verse 10, that we have not sinned. Sounds like hairsplitting, but there is a difference. How do we know? By the next part of the verse: "We make Him a liar." There is a denial of current sin in our lives (v. 8), and there is a denial of sin altogether (v. 10). We have not sinned; sin simply has never occurred which concludes that it doesn't really exist. This is a popular view, even among those who profess strong faith.

> While we try to convince others of our innocence, we have instead succeeded in deceiving ourselves.

The word *sin* has become a joke, and "living in sin" is heard more in the context of a stand-up comedy routine than a heartfelt conviction. We use "sin" in the titles of cake recipes, but rarely in sermons or counseling sessions. What have we done? We've made God a liar. From Genesis to Revelation, God's story is wrapped up in one objective: to redeem man from sin. If there is no sin, there is no point, and Jesus died a horrible, cruel, painful, unthinkable death for no reason at all. Our flippancy concerning sin has made it all a lie.

In many places we have stopped talking about reaching the lost and prefer the terminology "unchurched." We call adultery "a second chance on life"; murder of the innocent is hailed as "pro-choice"; media flooded with profanity and violence is rated mature; and drunkenness is called "a well-deserved weekend."

Moses saw that the people were unrestrained (Exodus 32:25). They were apparently under no restrictions while he was on the mountain. Anything goes. And Aaron was leaning on the same rationale we hear today, "Do not let the anger of my lord burn hot" (32:22 NKJV). What is everybody so upset about?

Dragons can become adept at rattling off terminology that seems to soften sin's ugliness, but relabeling sin does not make it any less poisonous than relabeling a bleach bottle makes its contents safe to drink. It's a lie that assaults the character of God whose Word says, "For all have sinned and fall short of the glory of God" (Romans 3:23).

Confess and Roll Over

So 1 John 1 gives us a vivid picture of sin, lying, and darkness, but as always in God's Word, no sooner is the rebuke uttered than the heart of God is pleading with us to repent and reach for His forgiveness. And it's so simple. Verse 9, nested right in the middle of the discussion, says simply, "If we confess our sins, he is faithful and just to forgive us our sins and to cleanse us from all unrighteousness." That's a dragon project; train it to confess.

> Therefore, confess your sins to one another and pray for one another, that you may be healed. The prayer of a righteous person has great power as it is working (James 5:16).

Accountability is a trendy buzzword in talk shows and self-help books, but it's not a new concept. It surfaces in our culture as a means to deal with addiction, the one word we do hear because we didn't care to hear the word *sin* to begin with, and consequently didn't bother to deal with it until it became a consuming and destructive monster. Pop psychiatrists and authors on morning talk shows didn't think of accountability first; God Almighty thought of it. We need to get our dragons involved in talking, not *about* one another, but *to* one another. Catharsis comes with confession followed by prayer. Moses said, "And now I will go up to the Lord; perhaps I can make atonement for your sin" (Exodus 32:30).

Why is "I'm sorry" so hard to say? I really venture that it's not but that Satan only leads us to believe it is. If there's a movie line that we've all heard more times than Bill Withers can sing "I know" in a chorus, it's this one from *Love Story*: "Love means never having to say you're sorry." Ryan O'Neal's character said it as the last line of the movie in 1970. But in 1972, in another O'Neal movie, *What's Up, Doc?* Barbra Streisand delivered the same line, to which O'Neal's character responded, "That's the dumbest thing I ever heard."

He got it right the second time. Love means having to say you're sorry frequently. Pride is often the thing that prevents it, and pride always spells disaster (Proverbs 16:18; Jeremiah 13:17; 1 John 2:16).

When sin has done its damage, there are two things that can bring about reconciliation with those you love the most and with God who cares the deepest. Those two things are the two words: *I'm* and *sorry*.

I have been hurt by people, and I know I have hurt people. Same for you? Some of the most precious moments of my life involved the deep-felt tender and sometimes tearful apologies uttered from quivering lips. Satan likes to rob us of precious times, so he offers substitutions. Stubbornness, years of not speaking, but also this: He sometimes appeases our guilt by convincing us that nice gestures, gifts, and friendliness will communicate the apology we would rather not say. Usually I accept this as an understood changed heart. But wouldn't we all feel better if we could just say it? And wouldn't it be more pleasing to God?

The words "I'm sorry" start in the heart, but the dragon has to roll them up to the lips and spit them out.

Rolling over really is a fundamental of obedience school. Roll over, dragon, and we'll all feel better.

Repent therefore, and turn back, that your sins may be blotted out (Acts 3:19).

TRAINING
POINTS

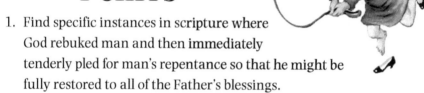

1. Find specific instances in scripture where God rebuked man and then immediately tenderly pled for man's repentance so that he might be fully restored to all of the Father's blessings.

2. In what contexts have you heard the word *sin* outside of a Bible discussion? Was it laughed at, glorified, or used in another way?

3. Research how gold is made into a figurine. How far off was Aaron's description of what happened? It is common to shrug off our sin with a short synopsis of this type, but when we look at it honestly, there are specific and sometimes deliberate steps that occur, just as steps occur in making a gold image. What are some of those steps that occur but we often dismiss?

4. Look up James 5:16 in several translations. Memorize it in your favorite English wording this week, and repeat it every day.

5. Do Aaron's words, "Do not let the anger of my lord burn hot," remind you of popular rhetoric? What are some similar phrases we hear often in our culture?

6. Do you think there is a difference in "no sin" in 1 John 1:8 and "not sinned" in verse 10? If so, do you think it is the same distinction made in this chapter, or is there another explanation?

7. Tell a funny story about a stain, burn, or other household disaster that the family covered up instead of removed. Is it still there? Make spiritual application in your discussion about what is removed from our lives and what is merely covered up.

8. Read the following verses: Proverbs 13:10; Proverbs 16:18; Jeremiah 13:17; Daniel 4:37; Mark 7:22–23; 1 John 2:16. Is there anything good about pride? Which of these verses stands out to you as the most alarming warning about pride? Find another Bible passage not mentioned that communicates the danger of pride in either more troubling language or entails disastrous results of it for a specific Bible character.

9. Our discussion of 1 John 1 begins in verse 6. What, in verses 1–5, strengthens the discourse following them?

10. *Sin* is reframed by prettier words. Among those listed in this chapter are *maturity* and *choice*. Be attentive this week to society's nicknames, and add to this list of misnomers.

11. "The Lord relented from the disaster that he had spoken of bringing on his people" (Exodus 32:14). How should this impact our prayers for the lost?

12. It has been said the people broke at least half of the Ten Commandments while Moses was on the mountain. Read the account in Exodus
32 and find the commands that were violated.

13. This chapter claims that redemption from sin is the theme of the Bible
from Genesis to Revelation, and indeed, all scripture before Jesus' life
and death points toward Him, and all after points back to Him. Go
to Luke 1 and 2 and find the context of the word *redemption* from the
very beginning of His earthly infant life.

14. Put a blindfold on a person in your group study. Have her draw a
picture of sunshine, a light bulb, and a candle. What are the results?
When we are walking in darkness and trying to give others a picture
of light, how distorted is it?

15. Repentance of sin and confession of sin are two different things. Can
one exist without the other? Is one of any value without the other?

THE TAIL END

And Speaking of Vacuuming and Bleach . . .

The trees are beginning to sprout leaves again. The grass is a lush green, and dandelions are popping up faster than zits in middle school. The meadows call for us to play between refreshing spring showers. Who wants to be the first to fly a kite in a brisk spring wind or make a daisy chain in the sunshine? It's picnic weather, and we're one day closer to wading in the creek.

And then it happens. Someone mentions it every year. There is a killjoy in every group, and she is the first to utter the words "spring cleaning." You have to wonder what diabolical creature first thought of this, and you have to question a society in which it caught on.

In the commercials, it actually does look fun. Someone opens a bottle of lemon-scented cleaner, and butterflies gracefully dance out of it. What they don't tell us is that it's because no one could stand to be contained in a bottle that smells like that, and they were waiting for the lid to open as if it were the exit door for Alcatraz. I rarely spend an entire day wiping down furniture, mopping floors, and scrubbing tile, but as sure as I do, someone comes in and says, "What happened? This place smells like an institution."

And that's a person who lives here. No one else ever sees my house when it's clean. I can clean as if Martha Stewart is coming with an entourage of *Good Housekeeping* photographers. I finish off each room with fresh bouquets on doily-topped tables and scented candles lit in every corner, and do you know what happens? As I am pulling St. Patrick's Day cookies out of the oven to grace the scene, someone gets cut or burned or has an internal organ rupture, and we rush to the emergency room while a demolition crew apparently invades the house for a practice session before we can return.

But then when my house is in full flare for Mess Fest Golden Anniversary Edition, a visiting preacher follows us home for lunch, or kids in mismatched pajamas at 2:30 in the afternoon run to the window and say, "Did Uncle Cecil get a new car?" We start hiding things as if there is some kind of hope that one of the guests will get a leg cramp that will slow them down on the sidewalk, and with a near miss, they'll be unaware that Chernobyl apparently happened in our den. We know that if any of the guests ask to use the microwave or retrieve a blanket from the chest, we're doomed. Those places are now full of random stacks of mail, Pop-Tart pieces, and odd shoes.

I usually blush and say, "Come on in and sit down if you can find a place to sit. I'm sorry it's such a mess," but one of my relatives (who would want to remain nameless) saves such apologies and simply shakes her head saying, "The maid didn't come."

I've never had the money reserved for a maid, but I remember my mother trying it a few times. It was awful. We cleaned and cleaned each time prior to the maid's arrival so she wouldn't have to see the house was such a wreck.

So what is it about spring that makes us plunge into a cleaning frenzy? I guess it's March madness. We're stir-crazy from winter sit-ins to the degree we can be entertained by stringing sheets on the line or beating a rug on the porch to the tune of "Three Blind Mice." Something drives us to think it will be fun, and then something wakens in us the realization that we had more fun than this on vaccination day.

My mother used to make us tackle the corner cobwebs each spring. She tied a dust rag to the end of the broom, and we swept the ceilings instead of the floors. But brooms were made to be swords . . . and guitars . . . and high-energy dance partners. I found out that there is nothing that can bring

I think I may know why Mr. Clean is bald.

the fury out of a generally sweet-dispositioned matriarch quite like redistributing the dust you just attained from the ceiling. I'm not saying she was out of control; I'm just saying I found out something else brooms are for, and I think I may know why Mr. Clean is bald.

Someone once told me that when a room is freshly painted, the walls are now clean. Hmmm, I'm looking around struggling with how I'm ever going to clean this desk, and these shelves, and this pantry, and the fireplace, and the playroom, and I wonder . . . How much does a gallon of paint cost?

(Originally printed in *Christian Woman* magazine, M/A 2016)

Train Your Dragon to FETCH

Be Evangelistic

Key Scriptures
Romans 3:23; Acts 8–9; Luke 15:10;
Matthew 16:26; John 4

I've never had a dog that brought a newspaper or a tennis ball or a Frisbee back when I threw it. I have had dogs that brought dead rodents up to my door, or clothes from the neighbor's line, or the garbage I put by the side of the road. But I do know that more sophisticated fetching dogs exist because I see them on TV. They've been trained to fetch, and once they have, they somehow find it so rewarding that they can't stop.

It's the same for our dragons. Learning to fetch what has been tossed away—the human soul—becomes so rewarding that once we have fetched that first person, brought her to the Master she was separated from, the joy is so immense that we want to do it again and again.

Conquer the Fear of Fetching

Most of our dragons, untrained, have a fear of fetching. The task seems overwhelming. The world population is over seven billion, and all of them need the gospel (Romans 3:23). It's a number I can't even comprehend, much less begin to approach with a Bible study. Imagine if you were trying to train a pet to fetch, and you threw out seven billion balls. It would be too overwhelming; nothing would be accomplished, other than perhaps making it into the *Guinness Book of World Records* for the largest ball drop and the most confused dog. We don't start with seven billion in fetching lessons. We don't even start with seven. We start with one.

God has a fascination with one. As humans, we overlook one for the big numbers. No one ever had an itch to drive a car that will go one mile an hour. No one wants a device with only one gigabyte of storage, we're not interested in flying one foot above sea level, and no one makes the cover of *Fortune* by having a one-dollar bank account. Consequently, in our churches, we want to see the numbers on the board, and they had better be big ones.

Yes, like everyone else, I do hope and pray the number of converts and faithful Christians multiplies. We do want to see a big number, but the way a number enlarges is by the addition of one, and one, and one more. In God's eyes, each soul alone is valuable enough to cause the voluntary bloodshed of His only Son.

> So the Lord said to him, "Arise and go to the street called Straight, and inquire at the house of Judas for one called Saul of Tarsus, for behold, he is praying" (Acts 9:11 NKJV).

Fetching Focus

In training our dragons to fetch, we must focus their attention on one. In Acts 8 an angel of the Lord directs Philip, who had just drawn a large crowd while preaching in Samaria (8:5–6), toward Gaza, a desert place (v. 26). Where's the crowd now? He was further instructed by the Spirit to catch up to one chariot, and when he did, he climbed up in it for a Bible study with one man. It probably wouldn't be the strategy most churches would invest in—one person on a road in a desert, one person en route to an important job, one person who was puzzling over one passage. The result was one person immersed into Christ for forgiveness of sins and eternal salvation, and we know that "there is joy before the angels of God over one sinner who repents" (Luke 15:10).

In the very next chapter, the Lord does the very same thing again. This time he sends Ananias to look for one, Saul of Tarsus. Really? One? Especially that one! Saul of Tarsus was the one strongly opposed to Christianity, ravaging the church (Acts 8:3), breathing threats and murders against the followers (9:1). He was on a manhunt, prepared to tie up anyone associated with this religious movement (9:2).

Ananias' hesitancy was understandable but not excusable. We have those around us who are strongly opposed to religion, calling the church phone and threatening to involve authorities if we don't quit it with all this literature. They're the ones we pray for. They're the ones we keep looking for ways to show kindness to and open the doors of their sealed-up desperate hearts.

Aren't we glad that God had the wisdom to direct Ananias to just one person? Especially that one! My New Testament sure would be a lot skinnier if it were missing the thirteen books written by Paul, that one who used to be Saul—before Ananias showed up. He taught, guided, and strengthened the churches of the first century, and His inspired words are still teaching, guiding, and strengthening me today.

> What man of you, having a hundred sheep, if he has lost one of them, does not leave the ninety-nine in the open country, and go after the one that is lost, until he finds it? (Luke 15:4).

Dragon Essential for Fetching

So where do we start? One thing is sure. We can't do it without our dragon. The tongue gets so much attention in sermons and lesson books because of its propensity to explode, but the amount of good our tongues can do is immeasurable. The value of a soul is beyond compare (Matthew 16:26), and it blows my mind to think that a nearby soul is teetering on the brink of eternal destruction or eternal life and can be affected by the words I say . . . or don't say. We sing hymns that plead "Will you not tell it today?"; "You never mentioned Him to me"; and "Ring the message out"; all attesting to the golden opportunity and responsibility of our tongues.

Our dragons, like the well-trained dog, ought to be fetching one precious soul at a time, rather than bringing up garbage, dragging up the neighbor's dirty laundry, and reviving rodents that are supposed to be dead.

We've looked at a couple of conversion episodes in the New Testament that illustrate the value of *one*. It didn't begin and end there. For the next couple of thousands of years, God has been using the same strategy to bring souls to redemption: one of His sheep fetching one of His lost. And just as a symphony orchestra consists of individuals focusing on one instrument, God's orchestration has used these sole-fetched lives to impact the entire symphony. Take a look at some examples.

Examples of Fetching "One"

Diane

Diane was divorced and struggling to raise her seven-year-old son, who had a "best friend" at school named Nathan. One day, Nathan's mother, Kay, invited the friend to come to church with their family, and also asked if Diane would like to join them. She did. When Diane was given the opportunity to fill out a visitor card, she checked a little box next to "Would like to study the Bible." A few weeks later, she was baptized into Christ. Today, she is a dorm mom to hundreds of girls at a critical time of their lives at a Christian college. The seven-year-old, now thirty-four, worked the past twelve years in the publication of a Christian periodical circulating to over a million homes. Who knew?

Brian

Brian nervously asked his high school crush to the prom. She thanked him for the invitation but said that dancing didn't fit with the convictions of her faith. He had never heard anyone say that, and when he found out that she attended worship twice each Sunday and Bible class each Wednesday, he thought that was radical, and yet her personality was not radical at all. As he became more curious about what made her tick that way, he found himself immersed in study not only with her but also her parents. A short time later, he was baptized into Christ. Though he and she eventually parted ways, the more he studied, the more he determined to attend a Christian college to prepare him for ministry, and he continues to preach today, along with his two sons and a son-in-law. Who knew?

Clifford

The local doctors had done all they could do for Clifford. The year was 1944, and it was time to board a northbound train from a small town in Alabama. If anyone could perform the needed surgery, it was the medical staff at Johns Hopkins in Baltimore. It would make history as the largest head surgery to date. As the day drew near, Clifford's wife grew nervous and his parents walked the floor. But there was that nice couple at the church of Christ who offered to babysit Clifford's toddler son.

A year earlier, Clifford's mother, Mattie, had been invited to come along one night when one of her relatives was headed to church. She learned the gospel within a short time and was immersed into Christ for the forgiveness of sins and added to His church.

Now that this medical crisis was at hand, her new church family was rallying in support. It impacted Mattie's family, so her sons, in-laws, and daughter ultimately decided to give their lives to Christ as well, followed by her husband who became an elder in the church.

Today, at least fifteen of their descendants preach the gospel. Who knew?

Tami

Tami took a job at the discount store. She noticed the guy who stocked in the department was kind of cute, but she noticed something else. When all the other employees were on break, their language was pretty much identical, laced with curse words and off-color humor attempts.

Who was this one guy who seemed to talk as much as the rest of them, was full of laughter and fun, only without needing to be bleeped? I guess she glanced his way a little extra to see if he ever let his guard down, because pretty soon she saw him glancing back. Conversation eventually led to dating scenarios where she became fascinated with the scriptures that underlay his Christian behavior. Today they raise five children together in the Lord as he works in ministry and self-employment. Who knew?

Troy

Troy opened the doors of his low-rent apartment to see twelve people on the ground, handcuffed. He had been a little annoyed that his video gaming was interrupted by the kicking in of the door next to him, and voices yelling, "Get on the ground!" But he was not too surprised. There had been two murders there before. It was the life he knew. He had not been to church for years, mostly because the sermons he remembered hearing as a child didn't make sense to him. But now his apartment butted up against church property. He'd go in and give it a try; why not? It wasn't exactly the sermon you would handpick for a visitor that day, but sometimes God in His providence is involved in the picking. It was an explanation of the miraculous age, its purpose, and its completion. It made much more sense to Troy than anything he had heard before, so it was bait to come back. The sermon was working on his reasoning, but it takes more than a preacher dragon to work with a soul. There were several dragons who spoke to Troy, but one bold one looked past Troy's rough-edged exterior and asked him to study. That's all it took. Troy was soon baptized and is now active in teaching, leading singing, and interpreting sermons in sign language for the deaf. Who knew?

Paul and Uschi

No one was home when the teens knocked on Paul and Uschi's door. Not only that, but they lived on top of a mountain, and the campaigners had climbed the long driveway in the July sun. Oh well, at least they had a literature packet to leave before walking away disappointed. A year passed, and the campaigners returned once again to help the congregation distribute invitations to a gospel meeting. They climbed the long ascent again, and this time there was an answer to the knock at the door. "Oh yeah," Paul said, "did you come last summer and leave a packet like this? We read it. When's the meeting again? We'll see if we can make it one night." Lots of people promised as much, but Paul and Uschi delivered. They were so fascinated with the truths they were finding in the scriptures that they came back the next night, and the next, until on the final night of the meeting, Uschi knew without a doubt she wanted to be baptized right then for the forgiveness of her sins. Paul pondered and studied a few weeks more before arriving at the same decision. It was only one house, and so far up the hill, and no one was even home. Who knew?

Kathy

Kathy, who had grown up in a children's home, struggled with loneliness. And her husband's new job had landed them in unfamiliar territory. Though full of wit and exuberance, she found herself leery of initiating friendships in this new town, far from any family and many miles from her comfort zone. But she took a bold step; she decided to join a bridge club for a little social interaction. One of those bridge players was a New Testament Christian who decided to use her dragon for more than just a bridge game.

Kathy answered the phone one evening to hear the following: "Hey, Kathy, we have Bible study on Wednesday nights and I really think you'd like it. I'll be there to pick you up in five minutes." And then there was a click. It was a great breed of dragon. One who knew the importance of boldness paired with brevity. It reminds me of the Samaritan woman's dragon in John 4. She said "Come, see a man who told me all that I ever did," and I think some people were there in five minutes.

Fast forward a few decades. I sat in Kathy's home where she changed the furniture out every few months so she could give young couples "new" and nice things. She was an elder's wife now, her home was a hub of fellowship and activity. She taught and served, and had a monthly section of her budget simply called "give away." She was one of the kindest, most generous, and fun people I knew. We were laughing and talking when the phone rang, and after a brief conversation, she came to me dead serious and said, "Make yourself at home. We have a young couple in crisis that needs our help and prayers. We've got to go." And she was gone. Kathy embodies the kind of Christian I want to be, influencing countless numbers along her path. And it all started with a brave little dragon from a bridge club. Who knew?

Scotty

Those bus workers of the seventies were exhausted. They had canvassed the entire subdivision when they entered the yard where a little boy was playing. "Would you like to ride our bus to church tomorrow morning?" "Let me ask my mom," he answered and ran into the foyer. Mom met the bus workers and decided it would be okay for her son to attend. Scotty continued to ride the bus for a few years until the bus had seen better days, and the program was discontinued. The congregation, not wanting to let any souls slip through the cracks, made sure that all the children who still wanted to come would have a ride. So Sharon and her family swung by in their station wagon to get Scotty three times a week. I don't know much more about her, if she's living or where she's living. But if I did, I'd go and personally hug her neck, because now Scotty preaches at my home congregation and teaches inside my home where he is husband and father. Who knew?

Clint

Clint was an altar boy in the Catholic church. But like any other little boy in his hometown, he spent many hours in the popular game room and hamburger joint. One of the regulars there was a man named Danny, a preacher in the area. Not only did he play games and shoot pool with them, but he also took a keen interest in their problems and gave them good moral counsel in those critical years. Time passed. Clint moved away, and as the pressures and transitions of the teen and early adult years brought with them every form of temptation, Clint pursued every pleasure, and yet still came up empty. "There has to be something more than this," he whispered one morning as he came to himself, much as the prodigal son in Luke 15, only without being sure of the clear path to the Father. He met with a religious leader or two, but human doctrine began to muddy things instead of making them clearer. From the recesses of his memory, game room discussions were pushing their way to the front. By providence much more than by chance, Clint was back in his hometown one day when he ran into Danny. They talked, they studied, and Clint was invited to church where a high schooler, Jeremie, was preaching just the lesson Clint needed to hear. Clint was baptized a few weeks later, and eventually went to preaching school. The rest is still unfolding as he, his wife, and their sons—the first of whom is named Jeremy Daniel—faithfully and prayerfully bring others to Christ in their work. Who knew?

Tyler's Parents

Tyler was veering off the path where her parents had been holding her hand at the downtown festival. "Where are you going, sweetheart?" The child was drawn to an *Apologetics Press* magazine, *Discovery*, because there was a fascinating dinosaur pictured on its cover. The dinosaur was silent, but there were dragons in the free literature booth that got busy. They made friendly conversation as they handed the mother a flyer about their upcoming ladies day. She attended it, as well as worship the next day. And the Sunday after that. Soon, not only was she baptized into Christ, but also her husband and son. We hope the same for Tyler as she nears an accountable age. It was only a dinosaur picture and a few friendly dragons. Who knew?

And he arose and came to his father. But while he was still a long way off, his father saw him and felt compassion, and ran and embraced him and kissed him (Luke 15:20).

God Knew

Who knew about the American soldier who spoke to the young German girl? Who knew about the survivor of the alcoholic father, about the lady who chewed on one lesson for thirty years before making a decision? Who knew about the radio station programmer who listened just a little more closely to the one-minute spots he was rotating than anyone realized? What about the couple in a hotel breakfast room who were casually invited to go to morning worship on the spot? Who knew?

The answer is, "God knew!" None of us knows before our dragon gets involved, whether that one sentence, those few words of kindness, that quiet invitation, or that chance round of dialogue is really more than chance. And while there are scores of people who ignore, politely change the subject, or even rudely reject attempts at reaching their souls, the truth Satan does not want us to remember is that we cannot know when one seed will germinate, producing an immeasurable harvest. And some seeds grow beans in a hurry, but some grow pumpkins from the seeds we scattered long ago and forgot about.

Bottom line: It's up to our dragons. God could communicate the message to the lost through mystic revelations and in theatrical ways, but He chose me instead. He chose you. Second Corinthians 4:7 says, "But we have this treasure in jars of clay, to show that the surpassing power belongs to God and not to us."

Millions are in need of the gospel. Get your dragon to fetch one of them.

Other seeds fell on good soil and produced grain, some a hundredfold, some sixty, some thirty (Matthew 13:8).

TRAINING POINTS

1. In Luke 15, there is a lost sheep, a lost coin, and a lost boy. In each case, there are also those who are not lost. But the ratio changes from story to story. Is there significance to the fact that when we get to the boy, he is one of two? If so, what is the significance?

2. If you have tried, on more than one occasion and with more than one person, to conduct a one-on-one Bible study, how does the response vary from person to person? Do you think that there is any dynamic that determines that response other than the recipient himself? If so, what?

3. Think about the community you live in. In what one event, like the downtown festival mentioned, might you set up a booth? Begin

planning now to be part of that event, to have a variety of colorful literature available, to station the most personable people there, and to pray for a harvest of at least one honest seeker. (Free water or lemonade is often a draw that helps event coordinators accept you as an exhibitor.)

4. Have you ever dropped seeds that you forgot about, and then some vegetable or plant sprouted out later? Similarly, have you ever known someone who obeyed the gospel because of an encounter with someone years ago? If so, share both cases.

5. What one person could you call or text, as the bridge player did, and say, "I think you'd love our Bible study class on Wednesdays. I'll be by to pick you up." What's stopping you from making that call or text right now?

6. What is your secular job? If you don't hold one now, what has it been? Do you generally work with millions of people at one time, or does your job focus on one individual at a time? If you were the only person involved in this field, would there be any hope for reaching the masses with your service? How do the answers to these questions help us realize that the gospel initiative is not too overwhelming for our involvement?

7. You can fish with a line hoping for one fish, or you can fish with a net hoping for many. This chapter has focused on the line philosophy, but what are the most effective ways of reaching masses of people with the gospel message?

8. Several of the true stories included in this chapter involve children. Is there a greater or lesser importance in focusing on children rather than adults? Give reasons for your answer.

9. We all experience days that seem to be huge exercises in futility. Share a humorous personal story in which a lot of effort was expended, after which things only seemed to get worse. It can be anything from a cooking mess to a road trip. Considering the exhausting mountain climb, and the impending long-term results of Paul and Uschi, how are our futility days sometimes less futile than we may realize?

10. Did you or your parents ever pick up a child to take to church? Where is he or she now?

11. Troy was a seeker who could have gone unnoticed against the backdrop of a sketchy scene. Do you think churches are trending toward safe neighborhoods and growing subdivisions and away from less desirable areas where lost and hurting souls abound? How can we better ensure that no segment of society is evaded by the hope of the gospel?

12. Much of this chapter focuses on stories of one person reaching out. But in each case, we can also see that it's a two-way street. In each case, there is a point where the lost individual takes initiative to also be a seeker. Find that point in each of the instances given.

13. We all have regrets of opportunities missed. Bring to mind a time you wish you had said something and pray that you can use this memory to wake your dragon to action at the very next opportunity.

14. Almost every instance given includes loneliness, hurting, or even despair on the part of the person ultimately reached with the gospel. What does this teach us about pain and the providence that goes along with it?

THE TAIL END

And Speaking of Rodents and Campaigners . . .

Few things in life are scarier. There is that one ride at the theme park that dangles you four hundred feet above the hot dog stand, but aside from that, nothing comes even close. It's the suspenseful moment when you find yourself on the outside of a stranger's door with a bag full of brochures that say, "The Church of Christ. Who Are These People?" It suddenly occurs to you that there is a possibility that someone may actually answer the door.

For generations, we have called it "going door-knocking," a phrase so ingrained in us that we think it's a verbatim quote from scripture just as surely as "forsake not the assembling" or "shun the very appearance."

The entire reason we are standing there is simply because someone needs the gospel, and yet our heart beats as if we are expecting a troll to come to the door, pick us up by the collar, and poke us in the eyeball. That rarely happens.

My friend Jim was awaiting just such an encounter at a campaign years ago when a huge man came to the door of the mobile home. Jim, small of stature and standing in the giant's shadow, swallowed hard and then opened the following conversation.

"I was wondering if you would like to study the Bible." Jim winced.

"Yes, I would."

"You would?"

"Yes."

"You would?"

"Yes."

I'm convinced this would have gone on for several more stanzas and refrains had it not been for Larry. It was because of workers like

Jim that the term "personal work partner" was invented, and Larry fulfilled that role that day, coming through when the other partner neither knew what to say nor how to stop saying it.

And so goes the round-up for the prospects. We come back to an air-conditioned building, a turkey sandwich, and a dry-erase board at lunch. Everyone reports how many doors were knocked, how many signed up for a correspondence course, and how many—get this—"film strips" or "cottage meetings" were set up. Somehow we all know what that means. It really means someone has agreed to watch a Bible DVD (that's the "film strip") or someone has agreed to study the Bible in their home (that's the "cottage meeting"). Even though many of us weren't even alive to experience the film strip days when bulbs burned out or overheated on the cottage coffee table, or projector operators dozed off and were now one frame behind manually turning the knob every time the audio went "ding," somehow we still know that this DVD we hold in our hand will forever be called a film strip by sixty percent of the membership. It must be in the Bible somewhere. We know, even though we have never used the word *cottage* in a sentence without the word *cheese*, exactly what the term *cottage meeting* implies. We also know, if we have ever watched these "film strips" more than once, that if anyone ever stops and asks us how far it is from Utah to Florida, we will know it is 1840 miles.

All the reports at lunch give us courage to face the afternoon. All of the reports, that is, except for Eulan's, who reported he had "six suspects." Had there been a homicide, and we had missed it?

We had always imagined there would be. On the heels of the morning devotional, there is, after all, usually an admonition to watch where you step, not to pet a strange dog (which is all of them), and to shy away from anyone waving a weapon. In Greenwood, Mississippi, we had been thus warned, and so it was fresh on the minds of two of our teen girls, one of whom bumped loudly into a lawn chair on the porch, and the other of whom screamed violently, sure she had just been shot at.

Yeah, door-knocking adventures are memorable, and I can't think of anything I'd rather do, once I get over the initial stage fright. It's fun across the street from your church building, but there's something even better about making a trip out of it. We pile on a bus and go four hundred miles away to help a church knock doors, and then later we host a group coming from even farther to help us do the same thing. Somebody could save some gas money.

But it would kill something valuable. When we knock in our own backyard, we get waylaid with schedule conflicts by day, and the routine settling in at our homes at night. On the road, there are no schedule conflicts. No coaches try to throw in an extra practice, no receptionist reminds you of your dental cleaning tomorrow, and there is certainly no settling in at night. We spend the nights executing all the plans we have saved up for "campaign week." They include huge pairs of underwear hung on campground clotheslines, "For Sale" signs on the RVs, and "Just Married" painted in shoe polish on the Peterson's minivan who are unsuspectingly playing a round of 1:00 AM Uno. They also include a lot of picking and grinning. It's an important part of the bonding that goes on that week—so important one of our elders remembered to bring his mandolin, but forget to bring his heart medication.

After the industrial nights, we are glad the next day that there are no manual controls on the "film strips" anymore. For me, the loss of sleep and tension crescendo about mid-week. Where some get emotional or irritable, I tend to be a laugher. This is bad news in door-knocking. I hate to bring it up, but a few years back, Robbie and I were taking turns "doing the talking" at the doors we knocked. Tragically, it was my turn, and somewhere between, "We're having a gospel meeting this week" and "We're also just offering some free Bible studies," I lost it. Completely. That's when the personal work partner idea came in handy. After several rounds of hysterical laughter in which no one was participating but me, and an unsuccessful attempted recovery, Robbie broke in. My only sober thought was, "What took you so long?"

The woman who answered that door was the only one who signed up for a "cottage meeting" that day. I guess there's something about that kind of joy that people want a slice of.

While that's a little embarrassing, I have nothing on Laura. Laura sat in a "cottage" watching the "film strip" with one eye, and a parade of mice with the other. The Pied Piper himself must have stopped overnight at this cottage on his way out of Hamlin and left half his luggage. Praying and remembering her purpose here, Laura was able to make it through the study. Almost. Almost and until one of the mice actually touched her hand on the couch. Laura jumped up and screamed in the middle of the Bible lesson. While everyone stared at her, what could she do now? Explain that it was the mice at the risk of embarrassing the homeowners? Make something up at the risk of endangering her own soul? Besides, what could anyone make up that would suffice here? There they were, even the mice's jaws hanging open. Laura did what any of us would do. She straightened her skirt, smiled at the strangers, sat back down and said, "I'm so sorry. I don't know what came over me."

Um, I think it was a mouse.

There are new kinds of campaigns now: medical campaigns, devastation recovery campaigns, and homebuilding and repairs. The goal is the same. The message is the same. The sandwiches and hot dogs and spaghetti are the same, and so are the underwear pranks. Only the methodology has changed.

I hope I get to do all of these in the future, but I hope I never forget the good old bag of brochures and awaiting the unknown on an unfamiliar porch.

I met Valerie and Gloria and Otoolie this way. They became my sisters in Christ (one of them in heaven now) because I knocked on their door.

And they spur me on when the trolls loom and the mice scurry.

(Originally printed in *Christian Woman* magazine, J/A 2010)

Train Your Dragon to
BEG
Pray with Passion

Key Scriptures
James 4:2-3; 5:16; Mark 9:14-29;
1 Samuel 1:10-18; 1 Peter 5:7

On the commercial, there is a well-groomed dog sporting a bandana. He couldn't be any cuter as he stands on his hind legs and whimpers, cocking his head to one side, and wrinkling his brow for dramatic impact. It's clear he's had more than a correspondence course in method acting. The commercial is for *Beggin' Strips*, and it leads us to believe our pets will attempt similar cuteness to get what they want.

Similar? Yeah, I've had dogs that would stand up on their hind legs, too, if you could manage to pull their front legs off the floor and hold them up. They only cock their heads to the side to knock stuff off the dresser—and forget about the well-groomed part.

How is it that they get what they want? We have a rabbit—don't ask me why—who is soft and fluffy and precious, but when her bowl gets empty, she doesn't submit a handwritten request for supplies. She slams things around like a saloon brawl on a rerun of *Gunsmoke* to get attention.

Dragons Amiss

Our dragons do the same sometimes. When we encounter problems we can't handle, what we really need is to go to the Master and beg for His help. But we tend to go everywhere else instead, slamming things around and even acting out for attention.

What's the root problem here? Whatever it is, it's an old one. After James spends the bulk of chapter 3 addressing the out-of-control tongues of the first-century Christians—high speed flapping dragons that lashed out and cursed—he opens chapter 4 by saying that when it came to the one thing they should be using their dragons for, they pretty much forgot they even had a tongue at all. He brings it all home to a generation twenty centuries later when he says, "You do not have, because you do not ask" (James 4:2).

But I *am* asking. It's a common problem. James lets us know there may be a little issue with the asking part, too. "You ask amiss, that you may heap it on yourself" (James 4:3 NKJV). Beggars stand in the soup line to receive the nourishment vital to their well-being. But some of us are marching up to the counter with, "I'll have a Double Whopper, well done, extra mayonnaise, and supersize it." We've left begging and started ordering.

For we are powerless against this great horde that is coming against us. We do not know what to do, but our eyes are on you (2 Chronicles 20:12).

Begging Specifically

Prayer is a dragon project, the spoken word of man to the compassionate ear of God. In the darkest of midnight, chained to a log in a dungeon, the dragon roars. At least, that's where Paul and Silas prayed (Acts 16). In Psalm 6, we read of the first waterbed, made that way because of all-night crying and calling out to the Lord who would hear. In the Garden of Gethsemane, in the dark of night, in tears and giant beads of sweat, our Savior pled with His Father (Matthew 26:36; Mark 14:32; Luke 22:44).

You think those prayers were specific? You think those met the criteria of effectual and fervent (James 5:16 KJV)? I have a feeling the psalmist wasn't brushing broad strokes covering "all those for whom it is our duty to pray." I don't think Paul was asking God to go with us "to our respective places," and I don't think Silas chimed in with "we pray this food to the nourishment of our bodies." There's nothing wrong with those phrases. There is much right with those phrases. But let's take our prayers to another level. Let's cry out for help to the One who *can* help.

Be specific! You're begging. I've never had a beggar come up to me in the parking lot and be overly general or unsure of his need. Let's look at some specific Bible beggars who fell down at their Master's feet.

Begging for Healing

Once an official came to Jesus saying, "Sir, come down before my child dies" (John 4:49). Similarly, Mark tells of Jairus, ruler of the synagogue who "seeing him . . . fell at his feet and implored him earnestly, saying, 'My little daughter is at the point of death. Come and lay your hands on her, so that she may be made well and live'" (Mark 5:22–23).

The parent animal is passionate like no other. The extremes he can explore on behalf of a helpless son or daughter cross cultural contexts and know no social boundaries. Each of these fathers held an esteemed position—one an official and the other a ruler. No doubt they had busy schedules and looming lists waiting to be checked off at the office. But you can't hold a position so high or have a schedule so busy that it would keep you from throwing yourself down begging at the feet of someone who can help your sick child. Two superiors found common ground with one another, and with every mother who has ever sat bedside to a seriously ill child, wringing her hands between wiping a wet forehead, whispering a desperate prayer in every breath.

Apparently at least one of these daddies had traveled many miles to find the Great Physician. On his way back from his begging encounter, he met some of his servants—it had been a day since he had spoken to Jesus, and he wasn't yet home (John 4:51–53). But his servants met him with good news: "Yesterday at the seventh hour the fever left him." There is no distance too great for a parent to travel for the sake of his child.

Begging for More

No doubt these two fathers held a faith that was anchored deep. But others of us relate more to the father of the boy with the unclean spirit. He too begged Jesus saying, "But if you can do anything, have compassion on us and help us" (Mark 9:22). The plea is moving but falls short in confidence. How many of us approach God for help with the shortsighted faith of "if you can"? For all the poignancy of the first response, when Jesus answered him, "All things are possible for one who believes," his next response is even more stirring.

> Immediately, the father of the child cried out, and said, "I believe; help my unbelief!" (Mark 9:24).

It's a contradicting statement that hits home.

We find ourselves in dire need of our God, and in the very prayer for His intervention, we throw in an "if." But here's the key. This man differs from the child of God who flaunts his doubts as an intellectual privilege or a conversation piece at some theological roundtable. He takes no time for debate but immediately knows and acknowledges his strong desire for more faith, deeper faith, higher faith. When your child suffers multiple burns from a destructive mindset, this faith is what you crave. Beg for it!

Begging for Less

And at the end of a bad day, a very bad day, a day that you would trade for a root canal or traffic court in a heartbeat, your dragon cries out to the Helper of days. Lot had such a day in Genesis 19. He had unexpected company. That's enough for some of us if the story stopped there. But that was the good part. His house was later surrounded by a violent, sex-obsessed gang of men intent on raping his guests and harming Lot. Now Lot was no doubt processing what he had offered them in a moment of fear—his daughters. What was he thinking? The gang had chanted the same old thing we hear today, their own version of "who made you a judge of right and wrong?" His daughters' boyfriends didn't take him seriously (Genesis

19:14) and had no respect for him. His city and everything he owned was destroyed as he was snatched by the hand and pulled out of a city God had marked for imminent destruction.

As he spoke to the angels of God, his dragon dropped to its knees:

> Behold, your servant has found favor in your sight, and you have shown me great kindness in saving my life. But I cannot escape to the hills, lest the disaster overtake me and I die. Behold, this city is near enough to flee to, and it is a little one. Let me escape there—is it not a little one?—and my life will be saved! (Genesis 19:19-20).

You can almost hear his voice crack and see the tears roll as he begs for something little. In the midst of the unexpected company of crisis, defeat, and misery, our dragons beg, "Give me something little. Give me something I can handle. Please, God, is there something little?"

Begging for Deliverance

Few dragons have the stamina or eloquence of Hezekiah's, especially considering the circumstances. Judah was the next tick mark on Assyria's takeover. The military powerhouse had conquered surrounding nations and had already begun conquering Judean cities. Their strategy was intimidation. Surrender-or-else was the tactic.

The event unfolds in 2 Kings 18. Assyria's King Sennacherib sent the Rabshakeh, which is a really fun way to say governor, who taunted King Hezekiah and his subjects from the city wall. Some of the Jewish priests and scribes, Eliakim, Shebnah, and Joah, begged him and his colleagues to speak in Aramaic and not in Hebrew: "Do not speak to us in the language of Judah within the hearing of the people who are on the wall" (2 Kings 18:26). But they continued to belittle God, to remind everyone that the other nations' gods had been unable to deliver them, to speak to them in vulgarities, and to do it defiantly in the Hebrew language.

At the end of the brazen oration, King Hezekiah sent for word from Isaiah the prophet, who in no uncertain terms assured Hezekiah of God's victory. But the Assyrian king was relentless, again sending a written message, reminding Hezekiah that no other kingdom had been able to stand against his military, and no other gods had come through either.

Hezekiah quit walking the floor and hit the floor, something we don't always do on the first cue. The text tells us he spread the letter out before God (2 Kings 19:14), and his dragon started begging:

O Lord, the God of Israel, enthroned above the cherubim, you are the God, you alone, of all the kingdoms of the earth; you have made heaven and earth. Incline your ear, O Lord, and hear; open your eyes, O Lord, and see; and hear the words of Sennacherib, which he has sent to mock the living God. Truly, O Lord, the kings of Assyria have laid waste the nations and their lands and have cast their gods into the fire, for they were not gods, but the work of men's hands, wood and stone. Therefore they were destroyed. So now, O Lord our God, save us, please, from his hand, that all the king-doms of the earth may know that you, O Lord, are God alone (2 Kings 19:15–19).

The Enemy's Dragon

Is someone making fun of your God? Is someone belittling His power? That's what happened to twelve-year-old Giovanni in a Florida public school. When he read his Bible during free time, the teacher demanded that he dial his parents in front of the class so she could tell them what he had done (Starnes, 2014).

Apparently, such schools are calling in the "Rabshakehs" for back up, and they're targeting the smaller and younger. In California a deputy went to a boy's home to inform the parents that he could no longer hand out Bible verses at lunch (Starnes, 2016).

Maybe it's not a teacher or an officer who belittles you. Some Rab-shakehs come from our own dens and bedrooms, across the street or across town, back home or await us at extended family visits. This week

I learned of a college student whose parents threatened to take away her car if she decided to follow Christ.

No tactics are off limits for the enemy. He will shout from the walls in the hearing and the language of the people. He will use vulgarities to increase the embarrassment and intimidation. And he will stoop to bright and colorful pop-up books for children. I was drawn to such a book a few years back because it was bright green and shouted fun with its whimsical title, *Flanimals*. I was not so surprised to learn that it taught evolution through its creative illustrations. After all, children have become the prime audience for the atheistic agenda. But I was heartbroken to turn the page and realize that a child who couldn't even yet tie his shoe could read the following in fun fonts and pop-out pictures, "One Flanimal thought that a weird creature called Grob, who lives in the sky, made all the Flanimals in one day. Mental!" (Gervais and Steer).

Such foolish propaganda is reminiscent of that of Sennacherib and the Rabshakeh. And there is only one worthwhile response: that of Hezekiah's dragon. There is no need for God's children to cower in a corner but praise God with a louder voice while we beg for His deliverance.

> And she vowed a vow and said, "O Lord of hosts, if you will indeed look on the affliction of your servant and remember me and not forget your servant, but will give to your servant a son, then I will give him to the Lord all the days of his life, and no razor shall touch his head" (1 Samuel 1:11).

Begging from a Mother

In contrast, when we try to handle it ourselves, it's like turning the blender on with the lid off. Take one look at Judges 17:6, the "I've got this" attitude, and then turn just two chapters over and see the full depravity that results.

But on the heels of despair brought on by godlessness, a prayer emerged that would lift the shadows and crack the door open for light. Desperate times call for desperate dragons.

This time the prayer came from a dragon so meek and injured that the lips moved but the voice was stifled. It was a mother's prayer. Those are the ones that erupt with intensity, no matter how silent. Hannah's prayer in 1 Samuel 1:11 was for a child, but she did not know that the fate of a nation hinged on that prayer.

> Remember me and . . . give to your servant a son, then I will give him to the Lord all the days of his life" (1 Samuel 1:11).

How often has a mother's prayer for her child had ripples far beyond the immediate? We don't know how much is riding on a quiet prayer for a little boy. Beg, mothers. Beg for the spiritual welfare of your child now and in the future. Beg hard amid tears as Hannah did. Your dragons are among the most powerful.

I bet a great many prayers followed the prayer we know about. I bet Hannah's dragon cried all the way to Shiloh, and the Lord heard. I bet a few tears splashed on the coat she was hemming on her lap every year while Samuel was away, but I'm pretty sure those tears were soothed as she lifted her voice to the Lord. And something else was going on down the road. A lot of Israel's history and our heritage lies in the words, "And Samuel grew, and the Lord was with him" (1 Samuel 3:19). Samuel became a powerful servant for the Lord in a number of ways, but one of his strengths was prayer. No wonder his prayer life was exemplary—he came from praying stock.

Begging for the Lost

Mothers, your example of prayer in front of sons and daughters may carry over into their own Shiloh and Mizpah and Gilgal and Bethlehem. Samuel was a prayer warrior before we even started saying "prayer warrior." In 1 Samuel 12, Samuel harshly rebuked the people for insisting on having an earthly king when their heavenly Father had so abundantly historically cared for them. No sooner had he issued the rebuke than he assured them of his commitment to prayer for them.

> Moreover, as for me, far be it from me that I should sin against the Lord by ceasing to pray for you, and I will instruct you in the good and the right way (1 Samuel 12:23).

What good is it to pray for those who insist on raising up kings in their lives, those who reject God's will and have chosen to be like the nations around them (1 Samuel 8:20)? Is it a waste of time? No doubt, far more heart wrenching than the scare of sickness, the sting of ridicule, or the weariness of trouble after trouble is the anguish of the one you love turning his heart from his God. Can we call out to the one they rejected? Not only can we, but according to Samuel, it's a sin not to.

Some interesting terminology is used concerning helpless man begging to almighty God: "Cast your anxiety," "Pour out your heart," and "Spread it before the Lord."

Cast Your Anxiety

The first is found in 1 Peter 5:7, "Casting all your anxieties on him, because he cares for you." Peter, the one quick to act on anxieties, was also more than a little familiar with the fishing routine. He knew about casting.

When I was a little girl, we used to hop into the car every time my daddy got an off day and head to Logan Martin or Smith Lake and sit on the bank for hours. We weren't so fond of the sitting part, but we would use any excuse we could think of to cast the line again. We cut our teeth on rods and reels, and we were trained in casting. It was the best part. We'd practice at home in the yard, resulting in more than a few trips up a pine tree to retrieve a lure. We'd cast a line to the middle of the lake, but when we'd bring along less experienced friends, they would just give the rod a little jolt, and they'd end up with a cork bobbing around at their feet. It wasn't really casting; it was dropping. It was still right there.

When you and I have anxieties, let's cast

When you and I have anxieties, let's cast them!

them! It's the best part. When you cast them as far as you can on the strongest shoulders of the one who cares for you, these anxieties aren't dangling at your feet anymore. You can quit worrying about them. Oh I know, we're still not fond of the sitting part, but we can rest assured our casting has hit a bullseye, "because he cares for you." I'm pretty sure from Luke 5 that we get powerful results from great casting.

Pour Out Your Heart

The second begging terminology is found in Psalm 62:8: "Trust in him at all times, O people; pour out your heart before him; God is a refuge for us." If you pour something out, it's gone. And you can pour it in the wrong place. My toddlers illustrated this over and over again, as if I didn't get the point the first time orange juice was in the hard drive. Don't pour out your heart in the wrong place. Some of us, teens and young adults in particular, are turning to social media sites, wrongly perceiving that total strangers care about our problems. I'm not against socializing on safe sites, but it's not the place to pour out your heart. The throne room of God is the place to do that. And just try bottling back up what has been poured out. It can't be done in the physical realm. Quit trying to do it in the spiritual. Pour it out before the Lord, trust in Him at all times, and it's no longer bottled up inside.

Spread It before the Lord

Finally, the third interesting begging technique goes back to the story we explored about Hezekiah. He had received the letter from the king of Assyria, "and Hezekiah went up to the house of the Lord, and spread it before the Lord." What is your trouble? Spread it out before the Lord. Show it all to your Father. Yes, He already knows, but get it all out there so you can both see it at the same time. Begging benefits the beggar, not the giver.

Cast it out.

Pour it out.

Spread it out.

Sit on the bank and wait.

Wait for the Lord; be strong, and let your heart take courage; wait for the Lord! (Psalm 27:14).

TRAINING POINTS

1. It is said that begging benefits the beggar, and not the giver. Do you agree or disagree? Why?

2. What about this statement? "There is no need for God's children to cower in a corner, but praise God with a louder voice while we beg for deliverance." There are righteous people teaching in hostile nations who are hiding their work, their praise, and their worship. Is it right to hide our teaching for the benefit of remaining in the country so that more souls might receive salvation?

3. At what point does it become necessary for our voices to be heard by the enemy?

4. List some examples from Scripture of both covert and brazenly overt operations that furthered God's cause. Was God pleased with both strategies?

5. For fun, recall a fishing memory from your childhood if you ever got to participate in bank or boat fishing.

6. Of casting, pouring, or spreading, which word picture gets your attention the most to let go and trust God?

7. A few instances were given of children being persecuted here in our country because of an outward show of an inward faith in God. There are so many more than this handful of examples. Do a little research this week to find and share other more recent instances of silencing Christians. Include any updates of proceedings in the case, positive or negative.

THE TAIL END

And Speaking of the Parent Animal . . .

Why couldn't I ever be grounded? It seemed like all the popular kids were always talking about being grounded. I had nothing to contribute to the conversation. Those of us who weren't grounded still showed up for the Saturday algebra test review, the raking of the church lawn, and our brother's four-hour pinewood derby in 104-degree weather. "Why can't I stay home like the cool kids?" I would say.

"They're in trouble; you're a good kid."

But then whenever I did try something that would have gotten anyone else grounded, I went scot-free, if scot-free means the state of scraping mold out of the refrigerator and picking up enough cockleburs to velcro a Boeing 757 to the wall.

It seems that all the other parents were reading whatever the popular psychologists were writing at the time concerning discipline, and mine were still sticking to Proverbs 23:13, "Do not withhold correction from a child, for if you beat him with a rod, he will not die."

Every good Christian parent struggles with the day-to-day challenges of disciplining children. No matter how much they seem to have all the answers, they just haven't been asked the right question yet. They probably haven't been asked if Goo-Gone will remove staples from the leather couch. They probably haven't been asked why the laptop didn't come clean in the washing machine.

The deal is, we're trying here! We're reading all the good parenting books, and we're still paddling upstream most days with Cheeto-stained paddles. We know—we *know* there are firm discipline rules that cannot be broken in place for us, the parents; we just forgot where we put them when a crisis comes crashing through the unbreakable screen.

Rule #1: Don't Threaten if You Cannot Follow Through.
It's a valuable construct—one that solidifies a child's understanding of consequences. If a parent promises to do something, and then can't or doesn't follow through, the child quickly learns a lie, that there are no consequences for wrong behavior, and this can lead him into a long path of destruction.

But when you're staring down at a box of seventy-two energy-saving light bulbs which your child brought home to peddle off for a school fundraiser, but which have just been destroyed in a laundry room fire, you might say what my mother said, "You are never allowed to sell anything again for your entire life." I'm telling you, I feel a tinge of guilt every time one of my books is sold, and I usually get someone else to handle the money.

Or when the tuition for a class is slightly less than a Ferrari installment, and you find out there is an assignment that is still undone, you might say what I overheard on my husband's end of the conversation, "Get that thing turned in or I will personally drive three hours to the college campus and spank you."

The one example I've heard parenting experts use over and over in this area, is to never say you are going to call the police unless of course it is something so endangering, and a near-grown child is so out of control that it is warranted. But how about, say, if the policeman is already there? My mother was struggling with my preschool-age sister once in a department store. All children are born with the intrinsic knowledge that the department store is a place specifically designed for children to do all the things at one time that they have never been brave enough to do anywhere else. In twenty-five minutes, the child can initiate a complete breakdown of any dignity, sanity, or reason that the parent has acquired in the previous twenty-five years. At this exact moment, my mother found herself in close proximity to the store's security guard, and she said, "Oh please! Please do not take her to jail. I know that she will be good if you will just let her off the hook this one time."

I don't know who stared at my mother in more disbelief, my sister or the guard.

Rule #2: Remove Privileges.

By the time a child is in her early teens, she can easily make the association between abusing a privilege, such as visiting with friends, and having that privilege removed. However, while grounding is effective, there is something more effective. I call it reverse grounding, where the parent says, "You are going to every social event on your calendar: every party, every ballgame, every extra-curricular project. And I am going with you. And I will wear whatever I want."

Rule #3: Administer Discipline Promptly.

This means you don't wait until the television show is over or the birthday guests go home. It also means there are hundreds of parents who have never got to hear the end of a sermon. Or sometimes the beginning. Some get the administering process underway by the chorus of the first stanza of the opening song, which should have probably been "Sound the Battle Cry." We grew up accustomed to hearing a fifth part to the harmony consisting mostly of the lyrics "No!" and "Help!" There was a time in Birmingham, Alabama, when the toddler's pleas were ignored by the crowd until she yelled, "Is there not a Christian in the house?" and another time a little north of there when at the close of the song, everyone heard, "Help me, George!" addressed to an elder standing at the foyer door.

Unwritten Rules and the Final Rule

For all the written rules of parenting and discipline, both in the scriptures and from external sources, there are a few unwritten ones, such as saying, "Don't make me pull this car over," "This hurts me more than it hurts you," and "You know I'm doing this because I love you," to which my niece responded . . .

"You're spanking me because you love me?"

"Yes, darling, I am."

"Well, that's silly!"

This brings me to my final rule: Don't laugh.

(Originally printed in *Christian Woman* magazine, J/A 2015)

6

Train Your Dragon to PURR

Nudge with Encouragement

Key Scriptures

Judges 6:12; Deuteronomy 31:7, 23;
Joshua 1:6, 7, 9, 18

I f you want an interesting life, one in which every day is a new adventure, there's a surprise lurking around every corner, and the things you will experience are things that you have always only dreamed of, get a cat. That's because in dreams the wildest things happen, such as finding yourself playing with a yo-yo which dangles from a potato in a meeting of maybe the president of the United States, two or three of your church friends, the maid from *The Brady Bunch*, and someone named Angelo.

Having a cat is pretty much like that. It makes no sense. If you open the door to say hi, he freezes as if the *Miami Vice* squad has broken the door down and surrounded him with pointed guns. Then with no warning, he leaps to the lampshade before jumping to the ground and running the fifty-yard dash in record time.

Try this again the next day, and bring a friend to watch, and the cat will just barely open his eyes to acknowledge your presence, and yawn like you just finished reading aloud the last chapter of the owner's manual for the dryer.

When he has completely convinced you that he is extremely uninterested in you as a human at all, and you're considering how many lampshades you could save if you enlist him in the army, he curls in your lap and begins to purr. At that precise moment, you decide to keep him another day. He's soft, he's warm, he's purring, and you're pretty sure it's love.

Believe it or not, the dragon is a close kin. The same tongue that misbehaves without warning, knocks things over, and runs at record speed can also be soft, warm, and I'm pretty sure, loving.

When it's a cat, we call it a crazy mood swing, but when it's our dragon, we call it encouragement. Train your dragon to purr.

Encourage the Puller

Our little girl was four and in the middle of a tractor pull. She was a contestant, and sitting on a tractor not two feet off the ground with bike pedals, pulling a load behind her. We were at a farming festival in south Mississippi where we had recently moved, and in those parts, if a kid couldn't pull a logging chain before he started kindergarten, the parents sent him back. Mattianne was never much for losing, be it a round of Candyland or an Olympian sport, but this time she was lagging behind the boys. The crowd was unusually silent. For one thing, we ourselves were still kind of standing there in culture shock from the seed spitting contest and the moo-off. All at once, the tractor pull announcer said, "Let's hear a little noise. These kids need some encouragement!" All of us began yelling, "Come on! You can do this! Just a little farther! You're almost there! You've got this!" You could see an immediate change in Mattianne's progress. Every muscle in her face tightened, burying her eye sockets in determination. Her ears picked up on the encouragement and sent signals to her brain which alerted her muscles. Her sweat was the first to drop on the finish line.

Purring Enables Marriage Longevity

How valuable is encouragement? It's a necessary component to our emotional survival. There's a somewhat famous long-term research project concerning married couples, conducted by John Gottman. This study arrived at a vital ratio of positive-to-negative comments between a man and wife in order for the marriage to survive. The ratio then became a benchmark for the predictability of marital endurance or divorce. The accuracy of the predictability is astounding—93.6 percent! What? You read right. The researchers could predict who among their subjects would get a divorce based on the ratio of positive-to-negative comments in conversations they were privy to between husband and wife, and they were right almost ninety-four percent of the time (Fulwiler).

With numbers like that, we need to know the ratio, don't we? Here it is. For every negative comment a wife makes about her husband, or vice versa, there must be at least five positive comments to counter the weight of that negative one. The human animal thrives on encouragement, and the human dragon can provide it. We really didn't need John Gottman to tell us that.

Purring vs. Fearing

A defining characteristic of God from the beginning is encouragement. He said, "You mighty man of valor" to Gideon who was shaking in fear as he hid from the Midianites (Judges 6:12). Even with Cain, when I read God's words to him, I hear encouragement:

Why has your face fallen? If you do well, will you not be accepted? And if you do not do well, sin is crouching at the door. Its desire is contrary to you, but you must rule over it (Genesis 4:6-7).

It sounds like positive encouragement to do the right thing, and there will be no reason to be upset. Hebrew language experts tell us that the "you" in the "you must rule over it" is an emphatic form. God is expressing, "You can do this."

We are familiar with a similar shot in the arm for Joshua. In Joshua 1:7–8, God stresses that if Joshua internalizes and follows His laws, he will "have good success," followed by a beautiful promise:

> Be strong and courageous. Do not be frightened, and do not be dismayed, for the Lord your God is with you wherever you go (Joshua 1:9).

What a profound yet amazingly simple outline for encouragement. You can do this. Be strong and courageous. God is with you. It turns out that in addition to the three times God says this to Joshua in the first chapter, He also says it in Deuteronomy 31:23, and Joshua has just heard it from Moses sixteen verses earlier (31:7). That's five times.

Perhaps the information emerging from John Gottman's study is not startling at all. We had the same ratio in place over three thousand years ago. God knew Joshua was in for a challenge. The walls would come down in chapter 6, but Joshua would receive a rebuke in chapter 7.

When it came, Joshua was devastated. He spoke to God with torn clothes and his face to the ground. But it didn't do him in. We read much about the great leadership of Joshua beyond those pages. He survived the rebuke because he had been given five powerful doses of encouragement.

Five Times Encourage

Put courage in your sister, in your husband, in your child, and in everyone within your reach. We never know who is headed for Ai. I may stand face to face with that same person tomorrow pleading with him to repent, or he may be saying, "Get up" (Joshua 7:13) when my face is to the ground.

Over and over, encourage. Five times encourage! Use the same outline God used with Joshua. Use it for the child you drop off at the school door. Use it for the addict struggling to overcome. Use it for the new Christian. Use it for the missionary boarding the plane: "You can do this. Be strong and courageous. God is with you."

What John Gottman finds works for marriage, you and I may find will work for all of our relationships. Give encouragement at every opportunity. Criticize only when life demands it. Think about the very word *critical*. A critical situation when it comes to our health, our finances, our education is one that is approached with care, but it must be approached.

The outcome of the critical situation hinges on the attention given to it, and it is a pivotal moment for the future.

Purring in Critical Times

Will criticism—the kind offered in hopes of salvation and a future—be successful? It is our prayer that it will, but only if it is approached with care by the same person who has encouraged. Paul opposed Peter to his face because he stood condemned (Galatians 2:11). He had to. It was critical. But would it work?

Oh yes. We see Paul as a cherished friend to Peter after that (2 Peter 3:15). Why did it work? I think it had something to do with what happened fourteen years before that. "I went up to Jerusalem to see Peter, and remained with him fifteen days" (Galatians 1:18 NKJV). What an encouraging time the two must have had together. Think of a time you have been on a two-week campaign with someone, or think of that person who got assigned to your cabin, or your college roommate. If you could stick it out for fifteen days, it was because it was a time of encouragement that fourteen years can't fade the memory of. You know that person would be there for you at a moment's notice, and you'd fight off snakes and Mississippi Delta mosquitoes to help her.

Be steadfast, immovable, always abounding in the work of the Lord, knowing that in the Lord your labor is not in vain (1 Corinthians 15:58).

You Can Do It!

Encouragement gets us through Ai and back to our focus on conquering the Promised Land. I remember a very difficult and painful time in my life. I remember people saying, "I can't imagine what you're going through." That didn't help me at all. I remember some who seemed to blame me for the pain in my life. That didn't help either. But in the midst of it all, a friend knocked at my door, came in and put her feet up on the coffee table. She wasn't in a hurry to leave. And I remember what she said, "You're going to get through this. You can do this. God is with you." It picked my face up off the ground in an instant. I believed her, and she probably has no idea to this day that she had that kind of impact on my thinking and my direction.

Our dragons don't always know what they're doing, but when they echo the words of God to Joshua, they can forge a path for a sister to get up and get going.

Encourage. Train your dragon to purr. It can be the signal reviving muscles to action, and ultimately, shouting victory as sweat beads drop across the finish line.

In the world you will have tribulation. But take heart; I have overcome the world (John 16:33).

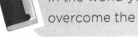

TRAINING POINTS

1. Just for fun, share a few of your frustrating or funny cat stories, or watch a short montage of cat video clips. How does this parallel the unpredictable nature of our tongues?

2. Who is your Peter or Paul? What friend did you bond with at least fourteen years ago? What is the distance between you, and what would happen if she showed up at your door tomorrow?

3. Have you ever had to confront a sister because you believed her soul was in danger? How difficult was this? Was the dread greater than the actual confrontation? What would you say, based on your experience, to someone who was gearing up for this?

4. There have been times we all have allowed an opportunity to pass when we should have encouraged a sister to get her life right with the Lord. How can we turn those regrets into determination? What concrete guidelines can we make for ourselves so that we don't let another opportunity slip by?

THE TAIL END

And Speaking of United States Presidents...

Every two years about this time, I am reminded of the first election. It was that time in America when George Washington was running against that other guy. I think his name was Arnold something. At George's headquarters, they were making signs which read "America is twelve years old. Isn't it time for change?"

Arnold came back with "Serious change."

To which George said, "No. Real change."

Arnold said, "Change we can believe in."

"Honest change."

"Change which never changes."

"Double change."

"Triple change."

"Triple change with fudge on top."

"I said it first."

"No, I did."

"No, you didn't."

"Did too."

"Did not."

"Did too."

"Did not."

"You're an elephant."

You're going to get through this. You can do this. God is with you.

"You're a donkey."

"I know you are, but what am I?"

At this point, Arnold knew if he was going to win the votes of the people, he would have to convince them that he was interested in the issues that were important to the people. There was, of course, only one way to do this, and that was with a plaid shirt. When people wear a plaid shirt, they remind us of our Uncle Jack, who stands for everything American such as the work ethic and Monday night football. Plus, Arnold knew that a plaid shirt was much better than a lacy shirt and a pony tail, which is all George had.

This is when George raised another issue which was pressing to all Americans. This involved walking through a field in slow motion with Martha, and holding hands with a beautiful child. This definitely tilted the election toward George.

The ensuing months were difficult for both George and Arnold, but in the end we know that George won, and this is mostly because his birthday is in February, and there was not a good holiday in February yet for department store sales, and so this would forever give us a reason to close government offices in February and head to the mall.

This bit of history is significant because it illustrates the rich heritage which leads us to the second Tuesday of every other November. I, for one, like Election Day. You get to go to the fire department without having to buy a spaghetti plate. You get your own personal space for two minutes (that alone is worth it), and then to top it all, you get a sticker.

Several years ago, I found out that even the bitter contest of rivals leading up to the Election Day can be enjoyable. That's because that particular election year we were located in a small town in South Mississippi. Up until that time, I thought the few weeks before an election were about commercial ads in which one person says that the other one is a rich trial lawyer and the other person responds by saying that he has never even seen a rich trial lawyer and if you say that he has, you obviously don't know anything about the constitution. But in Tylertown, I learned that elections were about meeting the candidates at the Dairy Festival and the Poultry Festival and eating lots of free ribs and chicken. I say, yea for elections! Except for that one time.

That was the day that the candidate was supposed to come to a barbecue at the park. It happens that having just purchased overalls for all four kids, and having a pair myself, I thought we might sport them at the barbecue, representing rural America in an oh-so-cutesy way.

Nobody told me. Nobody told me that, due to a weather threat, someone at the chamber had decided to switch the event from an outdoor barbecue to an indoor upscale luncheon. So by the time I found out, we were fashionably late. Fashionably meaning in overalls, escorted to the front row where the only seats left were.

So being on the front row, we naturally made a good photo op, one which yielded the opening page to the website of the candidate, who was running for and elected to a national office.

No one gave me the opportunity to say, "I am Celine Sparks, and I disapprove of this photo."

Aside from my main interest in politics, which I have already stated as being chicken and ribs, I am in all seriousness most concerned about the moral stance of the candidates. Sometimes, though, it's just a challenge to know. I'm not saying that it's particularly hard to get this kind of information. I'm just saying that it's sometimes easier to defrost your grandmother's freezer, this being the grandmother who has peas stored up from 1966.

I am in all seriousness most concerned about the moral stance of the candidates.

When a journalist asks for a candidate's position, he usually gets one of about five standard responses, none of which answer the question asked. It goes something like this.

"Mr. Candidate, how do you feel about capital punishment?"

"That's a very good question, and one the American people deserve to have answered. The American people are ready to have this answered, and they're not going to sit around and be ignored by my opponent any longer. If I go to the capital [the first part of your question], I promise not to let government waste and big spending go unpunished [the second part of your question]. No more Washington bureaucrats."

Mr. Candidate, do you favor chocolate or vanilla ice cream?

"That's a very good question, and I think the American people need to see consideration of this question. That's why I'm running for office, to give the American people the answer they're waiting for. There is too much government waste, and we need to get back to important issues such as this one, and that's true of eight out of ten Americans. That's why I proudly sport this plaid shirt, and I ask for your vote on November 2."

Does anyone out there understand any of these answers? I understand one thing. They are all collaborating to interrupt the best TV programs. They never seem to be interested in preempting the thing about who burned the most fat in a week. No. They only interrupt the good stuff like the $200 *Jeopardy* question which is the only one I know, and that's because the category is "Good Cheeses."

So who am I voting for? It will be the one who best represents decency, morals, the constitution, and family. Where's the guy with the lacy shirt and the pony tail when you need him?

(Originally printed in *Christian Woman* magazine, S/O 2010)

7

Train Your Dragon to RESCUE

Speak the Truth in Love

Key Scriptures
2 Timothy 4:2; Matthew 18:15–17;
Luke 15; Ezra 10:4

She redeemed herself. That mangy collie that could knock me over with her hairless tail when I was a toddler became true to her namesake. She was named Lassie, after the heroic dog on the television series. Lassie, the TV star, could carry on conversations like this.

Lassie: Arf, arf, arf, arf, arf, arf, arf.

Upstanding Citizen: What? This dog's trying to tell us something.

Lassie: Arf, arf, arf, arf.

U.C.: Something's wrong with Timmy.

Lassie: Arf, arf, arf, arf, arf, arf, arf.

U.C.: I think Timmy was climbing a tree.

Lassie: Arf, arf, arf, arf, arf, arf, ARF!!!

U.C.: Oh no, it seems a limb broke off and landed on a cliff overlooking a ravine. Timmy's hanging on by a thread, but his hands are tiring!

Lassie: Arf!

U.C.: She says "Hurry." Come on. Let's go tell the mayor.

Our Lassie wasn't far behind her. Our house had woods on two sides, and we played in the edge of them and forged pretty well-worn trails. But once I ventured a little deeper than usual and a little farther off the trail. I had no fears because Lassie was right there with me, rubbing her greasy mange treatment against my shirt. I was far enough in the woods that I couldn't hear my parents calling me or the siblings when panic began to heighten, dusk began to set in, and the search crew expanded by a couple of kids. I couldn't hear them, but Lassie, with her keen ears, could. She took off and left me, which was a little unusual for a comrade so thick. But when she returned, she had the posse with her. Unbeknownst to me, because I wasn't really aware of any danger, she had rescued me.

How to Rescue

Sometimes our sisters in Christ aren't aware of the danger, as they venture off the trail and get a little deeper in the tangled forest of the world. Our dragon needs to say, "Arf!" And sometimes when things are drastically off course, "Arf! Arf! ARF!"

Paul tells Timothy, "Reprove, rebuke, and exhort" (2 Timothy 4:2). Notice that Paul doesn't put the command to rebuke by itself. It's slap in the middle of teaching and encouragement. If we're going to rebuke, and we're going to have to at times, we need to get several things right.

The Right Rescue Ratio

This was covered in the last chapter. See the synopsis of the Gottman study included there. If wives need to encourage their husbands five times for every one rebuke, and if God encouraged Joshua five times before the rebuke concerning Ai, we should latch onto some very valuable relationship information here. The number of times we encourage our sisters should tip the scale over the number of times we rebuke them. When we are the ones who have pushed and prodded and cheered and hugged, our sister is going to be a lot less likely to close us off when we approach her about sin in her life. And we can't cram like it's a geometry final. We can't wait until we know our sister is in trouble, and then say, "Oh, I better go encourage her five times this morning so I can rebuke her this afternoon." We need to have a constant disposition of encouragement to all our sisters at all times, and not just so we can be sitting on ready for rebuke. We never really know who may be struggling and at a breaking point. A mild sentence of encouragement that we hardly think anything about may be a soul saver, or at least a day saver for a sister in despair.

The Right Rescue Research: The Person / the Word

A rebuke is in order when a brother or sister has sinned, and it is appropriate to be cut in our heart when we need heart surgery. But it's hard to accept a gash to our hearts when the sin addressed was not really ours. Paul opposed Peter "to his face, because he stood condemned" (Galations 2:11). But we must do the right research before assuming that a brother or sister stands condemned.

The wrong research can consist of listening to gossip, reading and believing an anonymous letter, seeking information from a third party, asking other people what they have heard, or just assuming based on a hunch or a feeling. The perilous thing about my using the wrong research is that while it doesn't mean a sister or brother is condemned, it does mean that I am. There are multiple warnings about this in both the Old and New Testaments. In speaking of those whose passions have drawn them away from Christ, Paul says "they learn to be idlers, going about from house to house, and not only idlers, but also gossips and busybodies, saying what they should not" (1 Timothy 5:13). Verse 15 says that some have already strayed after Satan in this manner. Paul plants gossip in the middle of a garden of the worst kind of depravity imaginable:

They are full of envy, murder, strife, deceit, maliciousness. They are gossips, slanderers, haters of God (Romans 1:29-30).

In addressing the church at Corinth, slander and gossip were among the things Paul feared most that he would find when he arrived (2 Corinthians 12:20).

But the right research consists of going to two sources; to the Lord and to the person whom you believe has sinned. We can believe a person has sinned because we witnessed the act, or because upon hearing of the act, we approach the person to find out if it is true. We go to the Lord in prayer on behalf of our erring sister and on behalf of ourselves as we need guidance and courage as we approach her. We go to His Word to zoom in on that guidance and to find support for each step we take in our rebuke.

The Right Rescue Recipient

When we go back and forth texting and messaging those who are aware of the situation, we have the wrong recipients. What does Jesus say?

If your brother sins against you, go and tell him his fault, between you and him alone. If he listens to you, you have gained your brother (Matthew 18:15).

The next verse gives us the rest of the story. "But if he does not listen, take one or two others along with you, that every charge may be established by the evidence of two or three witnesses." How did one or two who go along with you become fifty or sixty who have no intention of going with you, if you even go?

We're not sure we're in for that. It's a command we'd rather skip over and do it our way. In my daddy's Bible, the words are in red, and you know what that means. It doesn't mean it's any truer than any other God-breathed piece of scripture, but it does beg the question, "How much do I really trust my Lord and Savior Jesus Christ who died for my sins?" Oh, I'll take the grace that applies to my sin. I'll follow Mark 16:16. But when it comes to my brother's sin—my sister's sin—I'm not so careful to heed His words.

It is not until we've gone to our brother alone, and until we've then taken one or two with us, that we approach the church (Matthew 18:17). Could we get it any more backward if we were trying? Often, the very first thing we do when we feel our brother or sister's life is in jeopardy, if we do anything at all, is knock on the door of an elders' meeting. After all, their primary responsibility is shepherding, and they should know. It's true. It is, and they should. But only after we have done our part. It seems cowardice to dump so much responsibility in the lap of others who are already shouldering heavy burdens when we were unwilling to bear any responsibility ourselves. It's the easy way. But it's not God's way.

The Right Rescue Reason

Sin is the reason. The litmus test is, *If my sister met the Lord today, would her soul be lost?* If the answer is yes from a scriptural basis, then train your dragon to rescue. Understand that there is nothing else that matters as much—not physical sickness, not friendship, not family, not societal acceptance or acclaim. If we fear negative repercussions, we need to realize there is no repercussion worse than what is already in place. A lost soul trumps every other emergency and tragedy.

Note what sin is not. If your preacher speaks thirty-five minutes instead of the unwritten rule of thirty minutes, it is not a sin. Train your dragon to sit. If your sister teaches the ladies' class from the English Standard Version instead of the New King James Version, "Sit, Dragon, sit!" If a sister buys ten towels online for the baptismal changing room, and she could have gotten much prettier colors at the mall and they would have been cheaper if she had used the coupon for twelve, shush your dragon! A rebuke is not in order, and there is no rescue to be made.

It is more than okay to speak your opinion at the appropriate times. We have meetings to decide things such as themes and strategies for spiritual events and outreach endeavors. We want to value input from all and communicate openly as a family should. But draw a chalk line for your dragon, and don't let her cross it. Our dragons can blow a lot of steam if our idea isn't the chosen one, and all that hot air can wilt enthusiasm in a hurry. Let our rescues be true and valiant ones, and let them follow the rescue manual.

A lost soul trumps every other emergency and tragedy.

Thus, sinning against your brothers and wounding their conscience when it is weak, you sin against Christ (1 Corinthians 8:12).

The Right Rescue Recipe

Some of my favorite true stories are cooking foibles. I once made cornmeal cookies, which was the first mistake. But I also mistook grits for cornmeal, and the result was not going to make it to the final round of a bake-off for sure. Even I am not that Southern. I invented a maple pound cake because I grabbed the wrong bottle when I was aiming for vanilla. I also once followed a recipe in an old cookbook hammered out by a typewriter without a backslash key, so that ¾ read 3—4. Yeah, that did seem like a lot of baking powder, but I shrugged and scraped the can to have enough.

Kitchen fails provide comedy material. Rescue fails do not. It's crucial to follow the rescue recipe because a soul depends on it. Look again at the verse discussed in the opening, 2 Timothy 4:2, and see that not only are our dragons supposed to reprove, rebuke, and exhort, but we are also taught how they are supposed to do it: *with complete patience and teaching.*

Exasperation feeds frustration, and few good things were ever accomplished when the doer was exasperated and frustrated. It's common to approach sin with a "what were you thinking?" mentality, but it has never won many erring sisters back to the Lord. "How could you?" is not much more successful. It leaves the sinner with the impression that the very person trying to rescue the critical has no understanding of temptation or the tempter. Would you want a rescue team like that at the scene of your wreck or emergency? One with no concept of your situation?

I have found through the years, through trial and error and through listening to those I needed at the time, that there is an approach more likely to soften hearts to listen to you than any other I have attempted. It goes something like this.

1. I want you to know that I don't think any less of you as a person because of what has happened.

2. I want you to know that I love you dearly because you're my sister and nothing can change that.

3. I want you to know that the temptations you've encountered remind me of my own struggles.

In three sentences—and you may not even need all three—you have created a safe environment where sin, repentance, and forgiveness can be discussed on a level plain.

> Rather, speaking the truth in love, we are to grow up in every way into him who is the head, into Christ (Ephesians 4:15).

David was so far gone when Nathan approached him that he didn't even see the parallel in his life to that of a thief, betrayer, and murderer. I think if Nathan had approached him with those three titles, the outcome might have been different. But he sat with him and spoke with him, and when I picture it in my mind, I see watery eyes of a friend. Instead of David's resenting an accuser, he loved a rescuer who brought him to the statement, "I have sinned against the Lord" (2 Samuel 12:13). Mission complete. The very next thing that was said was, "The Lord also has put away your sin." Hallelujah! Mission worth it.

So here is the rescue recipe in a nutshell:

• *Complete patience.* Have the kind of patience with an erring sister that your heavenly Father has had with you. Some of us buy dried out onion flakes in a plastic shaker because we don't have the patience to peel back the layers of an onion. Peeling back layers of the real thing always brings us tears. Compare that with giving a little shake, and being done, and we're tempted to opt out of the real thing. Giving our sister a little shake and being done falls far short of the patience required to really peel back the complicated layers sin has built in her life to find the true healing, not just the flakey pieces. That takes time. That takes a relationship. That involves tears. But the mission is worth it.

- *Teaching.* Many times our sisters do not know where they went wrong. At times, they don't even know they are in violation of God's commands or in danger of eternal punishment. They need tender teaching, not from opinions or comparisons, but straight from God's word. Open up the Bible. Examine it together. Let her draw the conclusion. Teach.

Pay attention to yourselves! If your brother sins, rebuke him, and if he repents, forgive him (Luke 17:3).

The Right Rescue Response

When a sister or brother repents, it is the greatest joy on earth, and Luke 15 tells us there's a pretty big celebration going on in heaven too. But some of us are party poopers. Some of us shrug and think we'll give it a while and see if the person really means it. Some of us are convinced they wouldn't have repented if they hadn't got caught. David was as caught as a skunk in a pine box trap. But repentance is repentance. And no matter how far the sheep had wandered over mountains and thorny deserts on his own in Luke 15, the shepherd gently placed the wounded on his shoulders and brought him home. We ought to at least be able to walk ten feet to the front of the assembly and hug a sister on a pew.

The older brother in Luke 15 had the wrong response. He refused to go in to celebrate with the one who had behaved so disgustingly. Jonah had the wrong response. He loathed the idea that such an ungodly group of people could receive the grace of God through repentance. Let's look at a "church" who had the right response.

In Ezra 10, we see sin of the most complicated nature, followed by repentance of the deepest sincerity. There are tears, and the change of life is extreme. Shechaniah worded a response to sin that we should proverbially carry in our pocket. It was really directed toward Ezra encouraging him in his leadership of the matter, but what a simple and masterfully worded response as we stand beside the one picking up the pieces of a life crushed by sin.

This matter is your responsibility. We also are with you. Be of good courage, and do it (Ezra 10:4).

Your Responsibility. Dead On.

When the broken comes home with determination to change her life, we reiterate the personal responsibility this is going to require, but not without saying, meaning, and living, "We will be with you." We will call, we will pick up, we will drop by, and we will text. We will include you in every event, and we will share our own struggles so you can face yours, and when you do, we will say, "Be courageous and do it."

It's a job for a rescue dragon; a time when our tongues can be put to work in the most important of ways for a Christian. Don't let the petty dragons stand in the way.

Once in my travels, I worshiped with a congregation where there were two service dogs in attendance. They were there to aid and rescue their owners in case of danger. But instead of being alert to the occasion, they began to notice one another, walk circles around one another, and snip, snap, growl, and threaten. They forgot their purpose and became more protective of their own pride and territory than aware of the lives they were there to focus on.

I may have been on the road, but it hit close to home. May it never be that our tongues are too busy snipping and growling to notice the eminent danger of a sister hanging from a broken limb over a ravine. In times of spiritual peril, bring on the rescue dragons.

Him we proclaim, warning everyone and teaching everyone with all wisdom, that we may present everyone mature in Christ (Colossians 1:28).

TRAINING POINTS

1. For fun, share a story about a particularly insightful or heroic thing a pet of yours has done.

2. How complicated was the situation in Ezra 10? Is it reminiscent of any complicated scenarios in our culture?

3. There is a great depth of richness in the verses of Luke 15. Which part is the most moving to you in these stories of the lost and the found?

4. If you know a first responder, an EMT, or a servant on rescue patrol, ask the following questions:

   (a) What kind of training did you have?
   (b) What is a precaution you have to take that those without training might not think to do?
   (c) How important is what you do? Now, take those answers, and draw a spiritual application with each one about the rescues we make with our sisters as Christians.

5. Other than "how could you?" and "what were you thinking?" what are some automatic responses our dragons have to sin, which on reflection might not be the most appropriate ones?

6. Have you ever received an anonymous letter? Have you ever written one? You don't have to answer in front of your class, but together make a list of all the ways this is wrong and has wrong results. It might be a pretty long list. Now make a list of all the ways this can be a good approach. Did you think of any?

THE TAIL END

And Speaking of Cooking Foibles . . .

like them. Kill me; I like them. There's just something about the cooking shows that grabs my attention. I always come away with big plans for an elegant entrée in seventeen easy steps. Plans.

Am I the only person who cooks in, say, jeans and a T-shirt? Maybe that's where I go wrong. Everyone on the show seems to wear designer sweaters that came right off the mannequin and are just a little too low cut for my comfort. Really? You're wearing *that* to chop tomatoes and knead flour? When I watch the credits, I wonder if maybe I could get the dish right, too, parsley sprigs and all, if I had that many people assisting me, including one who is in charge of nothing at all but my wardrobe for a thirty-minute slice of my life.

Granted, the cooking shows have relaxed a bit to the point I can better relate. We have gone from the glorious Julia with the sophisticated accent (planets away from my world) to the frugal gourmet (much closer to my style except for the gourmet part) to the southern one who's fixin' to put it in the oven if she can get the thang to gee-haw. Match.

In the old days, there were very strict rules. You must make sure all measurements are level by running a knife across the top of the cup, and it must be the straight side of the knife, and if it's a liquid you must use a different measuring cup than the one you use for dry ingredients.

This is all pretty specific: "Slice the meat perpendicular to the grain of the fiber"; "When grating an orange peel (Does anyone do this?), be sure to rub the opposite direction of the holes"; "Gently rub the skin of the zucchini while holding it under water." And then, when you actually need very specific instructions, the chef says something vague like, "Just cook until it gets to the soft ball stage."

What does that mean? In my kitchen, I drop a little bit of the candy in the cup of water and then call on a few people to gather around to get a consensus. The consensus is that it looks pretty much like a slow tadpole. We do this multiple times until we literally have dropped enough of the candy to really make a softball, and figure we're good. We figure wrong, but we succeed in creating a burnt mess on the skillet that may never come off before the next Haley's comet.

To their credit, the chefs exhibit a colorful array of mixing bowls of many sizes, each one of them holding a single ingredient you then pour in a pan with everything else. Just wondering who's washing dishes here and what she has to say about this method. I guess I do this all wrong, but when I cut up a carrot, he doesn't get his own bowl. When I add flour, I usually do it—and maybe I shouldn't put this in print—straight from the bag. I pretty much serve dip from the plastic dip tub you get it in at Publix. What? Is that not gourmet?

When all the chopped ingredients come together in one place from their respective pretty bowls, the next part is just inexplicable to me. The cook no sooner gets the last olive in until she turns around and pulls the whole dinner out of the oven. Is this how they do it in cooking school? Sign me up.

Now that it's out of the oven and on a decorative plate with a side of leaf, everyone, including Al Roker, gets to taste it right there in front of everyone. And not once has anyone said, "Bleh, what did you put in this?" like they do in my family. When the ingredients are listed, I have to pull out the dictionary to translate. I might be able to make a tiramisu if I had any idea what a

I might be able to make a tiramisu if I had any idea what a mascarpone was.

mascarpone was. You have to know the language. You have to understand how to dredge and deglaze, to know the difference between farfallini and fagioli, and how to flambé while you fricassee. Some of us can grasp it better than others. My niece called from the grocery store to see what aisle she would find a "scant" on.

If you miss any of the details while watching, it's easy to pick it up later on the website. But not so when I was a younger bride. I would run get a piece of paper and pen (settling for a crayon and pantyhose cardboard) while the onions were sautéing, but I could never write fast enough to catch it all. That works okay when you miss an ingredient like parsley or a step such as "set aside." Not so much when you miss "Add 2 cups of sugar" or "Remove the packaging from the cavity of the turkey."

I usually fall just short of famous people standing around in my kitchen saying, "Mmmm, this is so delicious," but it's not like I couldn't survive on a television cooking show. I do have a few culinary tricks of my own, you know. The first thing I would tell a viewing audience is that if you are out of gourmet salad dressing, you can mix mayonnaise and catsup together. I mean, from a pretty bowl, of course. If you are out of gourmet honey mustard, you can mix mayonnaise and mustard and honey together. If you are out of honey, you can use pancake syrup. Bottom line—just don't run out of your basic condiments, okay? I would say all of this in a pastel sweater, and with very fluffy hair, which makes everything much more appetizing.

I could share much more helpful advice, but for now, I've got to get a jumpstart on supper . . .

If I can get this thang to gee-haw.

(Originally printed in *Christian Woman* magazine, M/A 2013)

"It is fun to have fun, but you have to know how."
—*The Cat in the Hat,* Dr. Seuss

Train Your Dragon to LAUGH

Take Your Medicine

Key Scriptures

James 4:9; Luke 15; Nehemiah 8:9-10

I f I were an animal, I would be a laughing hyena. They don't win any beauty contests, and no one wants one as a pet, but I think they probably have a pretty good time.

It can be extremely awkward to be a laughing hyena in my world. Because when all the other hyena varieties are sitting solemnly at a serious occasion, my laughing hyena fights every temptation to laugh at an unexpected mishap and loses the battle every time. It is awkward because my hyena tries to cover the instinct with silent laughter which shakes the pew but does not drown out the sound system. This works until suddenly the involuntary inhaling interrupts the silent exhaling, and it does so with a grand entrance (which probably should lead to a grand exit).

Yep. I'm a laugher. Why shouldn't we all be? If we are children of the Lord, we have an extraordinary joy that surpasses the surface kind. But God does not always speak favorably of laughter. The Bible instructs, "Let your laughter be turned to mourning and your joy to gloom" (James 4:9).

Why? Is it because God would rather we be miserable than joyous? We know better. It's quite the opposite. Those who are drinking in the short-lived pleasures of the world, partying it up on the weekends, and making sure all their ideologies mesh with the current trends, are paving a highway to misery. Such roads are often striped down the center with intermittent laughter.

But the Holy Spirit puts a big danger sign just before the washed-out bridge. Quit laughing. It's serious. Realize the severity of your soul's condition and turn that car around. Turn laughter to mourning; turn joy to gloom before hope turns to eternal loss.

Strength for Your Dragon

Oh, but once you do—once you turn that car around from disaster-bound to a sure hope in eternity with God—it's time for rejoicing, it's time for celebration far grander than in Times Square on New Year's Eve, and yes, it's time for laughter. When God wrote the script for such an occasion, He put it this way, "'Let us eat and be merry; for this my son was dead and is alive again; he was lost and is found.' And they began to be merry" (Luke 15:23–24 NKJV).

He wasn't the first prodigal to turn it around and start laughing. One of my favorite scriptures—my theme music, if you will—is found in the heart of one such narrative. Beginning in Nehemiah 8:3, Ezra read the book of the law to a wayward but penitent people. They wept when they heard the law being read to them. Their hearts were sentimental to a time before rebellion and captivity. And on this day, they were reverent, obedient, and solemn. But when the tears began, Ezra, Nehemiah, and the Levites urged them from mourning back to joy. "Go your way, eat the fat [I'm listening!], and drink the sweet, and send portions unto them for whom nothing is prepared: for this day is holy unto our Lord: and do not be grieved." And here it comes:

For the joy of the Lord is your strength (Nehemiah 8:10 KJV).

Did you get that? Our strength is not in numbers. It's not in health, financial solidarity, or even an active work force in our congregations. Our strength lies in joy. Not ordinary joy, not even special field-trip-day joy or Splash Mountain joy, but the joy of the Lord! The Lord shows His joy in Luke 15. It is joy over one sinner who repents (Luke 15:7, 10). Our strength is in the joy of being in the Lord and with the Lord with no doubts or fears. And look what unfolds: laughter.

Nehemiah, Ezra, and the Levites had hardly uttered the mandate to rejoice before mirth erupted. Mirth isn't a word I use every day. Or even every four or five years. But if we look it up, we learn that it's amusement, especially as expressed in laughter.

> And all the people went their way to eat, and to drink, and to send portions, and to make great mirth, because they had understood the words that were declared unto them (Nehemiah 8:12 KJV).

Laughing Dragons

It's okay to be amused. I am sitting right now in a hospital room next to my ninety-five-year-old father. He's struggling to breathe deeply enough. We're serious, we're prayerful, we're sometimes tearful, but let me assure you this day has not gone by without laughter. Both of us stand (or lie down) in a right relationship with the Lord. And the joy of that knowledge is our strength.

Everything is not going to go according to script in this life. The Lord did not promise us a pretty path, but a difficult and narrow one. He knew exactly what we were going to need in our knapsack, and one of those essentials is laughter. It's gotten me through the wackiest entrees life could dish out; what about you?

Laugh under the Mud Bath

I reserved the university van and took the play I was directing at the college on tour. We got to the Mississippi college that had paid us quite decently to bring our show to their community. I'm not quite sure what they were expecting, but I'm pretty sure what they were not expecting. They were not expecting the director to show up covered in the same Mississippi mud she had just got the van stuck in. Note to self: Do not stand behind the now twisted rear bumper when your accomplice or adversary—not sure which—gives it the gas and the tire starts spinning. What was I supposed to do at this point? Pretend I meant to? Run and roll in the grass and hope no one noticed? All I could possibly do was join in what everyone else was already doing—laughing. The laughing dragon always arrives in a better state, even when covered in mud, than the screaming, cursing, or crying one.

Laugh in the Sauna-Car

I got ready to take my daughter to piano lessons when I realized the only car in the drive was my son's eighteen-year-old Explorer. We were in the middle of a blazing hot, dry July, and it didn't have air. "It's only a couple of miles," I said. "We'll roll the windows down." I backed out of the drive, pushed the roll-the-window-down-right-now button, and nothing at all happened. In five hundred more feet, I called my husband and in a near-death raspy voice said, "What happened to the window button?"

"Oh, remember, his door doesn't shut all the way."

"But I'm talking about windows."

"Yeah, but when it doesn't shut all the way, the dome light stays on and the battery runs down, so I had to remove the fuse for the dome light just to be safe."

"Does the fuse for the dome light happen to be the same one for the window button?"

"I think I just made that connection, yes."

We barely arrived alive, so on the return trip we made a stop half way on the seemingly endless route for cold Mountain Dews.

There wasn't a single car in the parking lot. Not only were we not late, we were eight hours early.

The convenience store, called—I promise—Butter and Egg Grocery, took cash only, so I found a cup of nickels and pennies in the console, and we barely squeaked by. The first sip of liquid felt like Niagara Falls rescuing my parched throat. I set the Mountain Dew to the left of the driver's seat, got in, and tried to shut the door. But remember the door won't shut. I tried again and again until finally I gave it the slam heard round the world. Success! For the door, but not for the Mountain Dew.

I so felt like crying but wasn't hydrated enough for any real tears to fall, so we decided to laugh, and that carried us the remaining mile home to wet, wet water over crescent moon ice cubes.

Then our mouth was filled with laughter, and our tongue with shouts of joy; then they said among the nations, "The Lord has done great things for them" (Psalm 126:2).

Laugh in the Empty Parking Lot

When I was a little girl, all our gospel meetings had a daytime service and a nighttime service. Now that I'm a big girl, few churches have either, but the ones that do have the nighttime one. But there was that small congregation in a remote part of middle Tennessee that was going to have a good old-fashioned daytime gospel meeting. I talked my husband into taking time away from the office to join me. He was reluctant. I told all the kids we would get out of school early to go to the meeting. A couple of them invited friends so that our SUV was packed.

We weren't even sure where the congregation was. That was the first problem. We wound around back roads in Lincoln County until we were afraid we would be humiliated walking in late. But not to worry, we were just about to round the narrow curve and see the building. *Gospel Meeting* was in huge letters on the marquee. But there wasn't a single car in the parking lot. Not only were we not late, we were eight hours early. My dragon started laughing before the angry dragons could get a word in. "Apparently this is a nighttime meeting after all. I guess I was looking at Sunday's schedule, and got it mixed up with ordinary days of the week. Common mistake. People do this all the time, right?"

My husband's dragon didn't nod along. But no matter how much we analyzed the mistake, it didn't change a thing. So he said, "That's a good-un." And the SUV full of dragons laughed all the way to Arby's where we had a grand lunch instead. Not that any of them for one second has let me live it down.

He will yet fill your mouth with laughter, and your lips with shouting (Job 8:21).

Choose the Soul-Saving Door

Sometimes to console ourselves we say, "One day, we'll look back on this and laugh." The deal is, as big as this thing seems at the moment, I'm not so confident in my memory to get to the "one day we'll look back on this" part. Why would I want to wait to laugh about it then when I may forget it ever happened, especially when I could go ahead and have a good time now?

In reality, the more the person next to me—usually my husband—says, "I fail to see the humor," the more it becomes the only thing I can see. Laughter always beats misery, and God's design always surpasses genius. God knew about endorphins long before man studied, spelled, or pronounced them. He created them. Many moons later, man finds out that the muscles involved in deep laughter trigger the release of endorphins. And I say, if you can release endorphins through laughter or, as we also know, through exercise, hmm, I choose laughter.

Babies are born with three things on their agenda: eat, poop, and scream their heads off. But falling just a notch under these primary three is laughter. If it comes so naturally to a baby, why do we fight it as adults? I knew an adult Christian once who said it was a sin to laugh in a Bible class. I'm glad he didn't have book, chapter, and verse to back it up, or I'd never have a chance at heaven. Sometimes in Bible class, a brother or sister is going to read the wrong verse by mistake. Are we going to laugh and move on, or embarrass the reader in stone cold silence? The teacher's going to get his tongue tied once in a while, and when everything's going perfect, a cat will surely slip in the back door. Adverse situations may be on the enemy's side, but laughter is on ours.

Sometimes, it's okay to use humor for laughter on purpose. Laughter opens doors. And doors, when walked through, save souls. Well, Jesus saves souls, but we are earthen vessels (2 Corinthians 4:7 NKJV). Huh? Carriers. Messengers. And people are drawn to messengers who laugh. Ultimately the message is the only thing that can offer any hope, but how tragic it is when a soul never gets to experience the joy of the message because that soul can see no joy in the messenger. On the converse, often-times if you can get a person to laugh with you first, she will hear you out on a message she would not have been open to otherwise.

But we have this treasure in earthen vessels, that the excellence of the power may be of God and not of us (2 Corinthians 4:7 NKJV).

Be Like Jesus

We've all heard that if you're happy and you know it, clap your hands. What do you do, I wonder, if you're happy and you don't know it? As Christians, we're happy. We have every reason to be the most joyous people on earth. We have eternal salvation. Because of it, we can't help it; we're just fun to be around.

Jesus was fun to be around. Little children wanted to be in His arms. You think there was a little bit of giggling going on? Children aren't drawn to stern stoics. I'm pretty sure there was laughter the first time someone heard straining at a gnat and swallowing a camel. I can get pretty amused at it now when I think it through. And what about opening that fish's mouth, and there just happened to be the coin Peter needed for taxes (Matthew 17:27)? It was fun to be around Jesus.

It still is. Train your dragon to laugh.

Just so, I tell you, there is joy before the angels of God over one sinner who repents (Luke 15:10).

TRAINING
POINTS

1. What set of difficult circumstances have you faced, and in the midst of it, found yourself laughing?

2. On the other hand, what situation is proof of "we will look back on this and laugh"? In what situation did you definitely not laugh at the time, but looking back, you do?

3. In what situations, if any, is it wrong to laugh?

4. How do you feel about the Christian's statement that it's wrong to laugh in Bible class? Do you feel there are times when there is too much laughter in Bible class? When do we know that's true, and how do we strike a balance that does not rob us of rich spiritual knowledge?

5. Tell of a time in announcements, Bible class, or some other part of assembly where you struggled not to laugh.

6. What things make babies laugh? What makes children laugh? What makes you laugh? Is there a spiritual parallel to those things that interest us, or should interest us most? How is our spiritual development a metaphor to our development in the realm of laughter?

7. What verses in Proverbs show us the importance of merriment, celebration, and the right kind of laughter?

8. Which ones warn us of the wrong kind? What is the difference?

THE TAIL END

And Speaking of a Cat at the Door . . .

D id you notice in the past half century the shift from churches owning the preacher's home and putting it smack dab against the building to getting him as far away as possible in his own place? We have lived within walking distance to the building in three different locations, but we now live over eighteen miles away. There's a reason for that.

It started with our kitten who strongly believed in Mark 16:15, that the gospel is for every creature. She found us one Sunday night, and as we began to sing the song before the sermon, she belted out her own just outside the door at the front of the auditorium. It turns out she knew every lyric to the Meow Mix commercial, and she must have had a megaphone. As the sermon started, she disagreed constantly or heartily amen-ed while I pretended not to hear her at all, or at least, not to know her from Adam's housecat.

What a relief when she became silent after the first ten minutes. There was a reason for that, too, and it had to do with loose foil over a banana pudding in the back of a pick-up truck. It was heavily mourned at the following fellowship meal. Whose cat was that?

It turns out that cat was Emily Post compared to the dog we had at a mission point in south Mississippi. We could knock doors all Saturday with little success on Sunday, but we always had one hot prospect eager to beat down the doors, and her name was Beulah Dean, a dishwater blonde cocker spaniel. We tried it all. We fenced her in, put cinder blocks against the gate, and attached her to the crepe myrtle with a bungee cord. All to no avail. She obviously had been personally trained by Houdini himself before we got her.

So here's what we did. We deceived her. The building was straight across the street requiring a slight right turn to hit the driveway on target, so we turned left instead. We cruised a good mile or so taking in all the sights of the laundromat and closed bank, until Beulah Dean was convinced she only thought it was Sunday and went back to gnawing her leg. Then we would turn around and head for worship.

Until that day. We were just between the communion and the offering, and we heard a car pull up. Butterflies bounced around in our stomachs because we were so excited at the thought of a visitor. The problem was that Beulah Dean had also heard the car pull up. Imagine her surprise when she looked across the street, saw all the cars, and realized she had been duped. She quickly arrived on the scene and broke into panic, barking hysterically at our guests. I rushed out the door, leaving four unattended children to bask in Cheerios and half-pencil swords.

I had been so prepared for the greeting I would give guests when the day came, but all I could say was, "Sit down and shut up!" Someone quickly found out that the guests were Christians traveling through. Since we were a flexible small group, we adapted our normal routine and repeated some of the opening parts of our service that they had missed, which caused a lot of discussion on the Cheerio-sword row.

But before we could reframe our minds for worship, it happened again—the sound of a large vehicle coming to a halt outside the door, followed by a furious barking. I again rushed outside and convinced Beulah Dean that these people were our friends (even though I had never seen them before in my life).

It started with our kitten who strongly believed in Mark 16:15, that the gospel is for every creature.

This time it was a large recreational vehicle, and the people began filing out of it until their number now doubled our attendance.

These also were all brothers and sisters who had come to meet with the Lord's people on the first day of the week, so the public welcome was extended for a third time as we prepared to sing. When we thought they were all in and seated, we began, but they weren't. All in and seated, that is. As the group's straggler opened the back door and made his way down the aisle, so did Beulah Dean. And in the words of John 20:4, "the other disciple did out-run" the first one.

So again, I sprang into action. I tried to get Beulah Dean to follow me back out. I sweetly beckoned in whispers, I nudged her, I tugged on her collar. Suddenly the dog who half-an-hour ago would knock over cinder blocks to follow me, the dog whose theme song was "Whither Thou Goest, I Will Go," refused to take one step. She wouldn't budge an inch, except in the wrong direction. So I girded my loins and began shoving her from the rear until I scooted her completely out the back door. I am woman!

None of this was amusing to me. At the time. But I'm quite sure the inside of the RV did not lack discussion for the rest of that day, and if any of them ever appear on *Jeopardy*, they will have an interesting anecdote to share after the first commercial break.

Beulah Dean and the kitten weren't the only uninvited guests who've appeared over time. A snake stirred the scene once at VBS, and I remember telling him to come back next year for "Moses in Egypt" and we could probably cast him. And I will never forget the bee in the college section, causing those who didn't know what was going on to question the college minister's stance on just how the Spirit moves us in worship.

I have read about animal blessing ceremonies among some denominations lately, and I can't believe that people bring their animals on purpose. I'm sorry for my pet disruptions, but adversity makes us stronger, right?

It strikes a chord with me that the first human voices who glorified the Son of God after his birth did it in the middle of a field of bleating sheep while He lay miles away in a barn among livestock.

So when circumstances dictate, I guess we can do the same. I believe He understands.

(Originally printed in *Christian Woman* magazine, M/A 2010)

Train Your Dragon to COUNT

Count Blessings Out Loud

Key Scriptures
Luke 10; 2 Timothy 3:2; Mark 5:19

I saw a horse once on TV that could do math. The trainer would say something like, "What is twelve minus eight?" And the horse would stomp four times. I need that kind of trainer in my house. Because some days, we can't do math.

I was a decent student across the board back in the day, but once on a high school physics test, I made a zero. I'm talking about the big round circle written in red ink on your paper. Not just a terrible grade downward of the sixty mark, but the king of all bad grades, the feared number we shuddered to think about—the zero. It's true. Because the exam period was only an hour, and the problems each took what seemed like an unscheduled DMV appointment, we were only given five problems. I completed every step of the complicated procedure for each one, and if these had been literal steps you climb to my house instead of scientific problem steps, I would have lived on the 435th floor. The tragic part was, somewhere along the way in one seemingly insignificant place, I counted wrong on all five of the questions, resulting in, of course, the wrong final outcome.

I think if I had counted out loud, I would have gotten it right. We first of all need to train our dragons to count, and then train them to count out loud.

Count What Went Right

The Bible says a lot about counting. Abram believed in the Lord, and in a time before the law was written or could certainly be obeyed, Genesis 15:6 says that God counted that as righteousness. Paul says in Philippians 3:13 that he does not count that he has attained his goal yet, but that he's striving for it. James starts his beloved letter by telling us that when we fall into various trials, we really should count it as joy (James 1:2).

"Count your blessings" is not a verbatim quote from the Bible, and it's a pretty impossible task, but seeing that Ephesians 1:3 tells us that we have all spiritual blessings in heavenly places, our focus should be there. The reason I say it's an impossible task to count our blessings is that you could not begin counting all of your blessings from the time you got up this morning until the time you're reading this, even if it has been a particularly difficult day. That's just a tiny segment of our lives, and yet imagine the infinite list we could never see the end of should we begin counting all of our lifelong and eternal blessings.

I sit four days away from Thanksgiving as I write this chapter, and I also sit in a hospital room with my dad. We're all about getting out of here in time to carve the bird and puree the pumpkin. Thanksgiving holiday is certainly not a day mandated by scripture, but it is historically an occasion in which our dragons count the blessings afforded to all of us. No matter how much present-day opponents would like

When it comes to blessings, train your dragon to count out loud.

us to forget the original intent and no matter how much confusion arises about when the first holiday occurred, it is clear that early settlers had no problem understanding who was to be the recipient of our thanks. The 1619 English settlers to Virginia had a charter before embarking on their journey which required that "the day of our ship's arrival at the place assigned . . . shall be yearly and perpetually kept holy as a day of thanksgiving to Almighty God" ("Thanksgiving"). When George Washington proclaimed a nationwide observance, he set aside November 26, 1789, "as a day of public thanksgiving and prayer to be observed by acknowledging with grateful hearts the many and signal favours of Almighty God" (Hodgson).

No one wants to do away with the holiday. There's too much good food, a parade, and most of all, money to be spent. But those who do not want to acknowledge God have a problem celebrating a day that is all about . . . acknowledging God. Many are teaching our children that the roots are otherwise. We see advertisements and television specials in which the quality trait emphasized is thanking one another. And a cartoon PBS show I was watching recently, aimed at young children, called it merely a fall feast.

But not our dragons. Tongues bought by Jesus Christ acknowledge Him at every opportunity, in the hospital room or not, on a designated holiday or one of the other 364 days of the year. But be careful. Often those uncountable blessings we woke up with and enjoyed through the day are not the focus of our talk. We rarely arrive at an occasion and say, "Whew, let me tell you everything that went right with my day." But we usually can rattle off in grand style everything that went wrong.

Martha's Dragon Counted the Trivial

I think that's what happened with Martha's dragon in Luke 10. It simply forgot how to count. Martha was counting how many beans spilled on the floor or how many bags of flour she forgot to buy. I mean I don't have a chapter and verse for that, but I'm just going by what happens in my kitchen. She was counting how many sisters weren't helping her, probably how many minutes until everything was supposed to be ready, how many people would be there or how many seats she did *not* have for all of them. Sound familiar? She forgot to count that she did have food to prepare, that she had a kitchen to prepare it in, that she had a roof overhead, and that she did have the blessing of an earthly sister. And she forgot to count the biggest blessing of all. She forgot to count that she had the greatest dinner guest in all of history sitting in the next room. He was close.

Does our dragon forget that? Do we forget that no matter what hardship we may encounter, we are in Christ (Romans 6:3) and He is in us (Romans 8:10)? You can't get any closer than that.

See that no one repays anyone evil for evil, but always seek to do good to one another and to everyone. Rejoice always, pray without ceasing, give thanks in all circumstances; for this is the will of God in Christ Jesus for you (1 Thessalonians 5:15–18).

Count the "Small," Remember the One

Sometimes the dragon forgets to count little things. We can have a big thing going on in our lives, and I'll admit, some big things are better termed colossal: health problems, death of a loved one, divorce, marital struggles, wayward children—whatever it is, we become so focused on our one thing that we fail to realize all the blessings that are surrounding us and up in our face. When my mother's third grandchild came along and she was doting over him, the second one said, "I'm over here, Pump-pie." Sometimes we need to turn around and notice all the blessings that are violently waving, "I'm over here."

But then, sometimes it's the big thing our dragon tends to forget. Jesus said, "Martha, Martha, you are anxious and troubled about many things, but one thing is necessary" (Luke 10:41–42).

There is only one thing in this life that matters, and it's the next one. If we are in a right relationship with our Lord Jesus Christ, nothing else matters. If we are not in a right relationship with Him, nothing else matters. One thing is necessary.

We are so thankful for that one thing: Every problem pales at the thought of our Savior holding our hand and taking us to a place forevermore where there is not the first problem.

Remember that seemingly insignificant counting error that caused the big answer to be the wrong one on that physics test? Could it be that when we forget how to count in the seemingly insignificant places within our worlds, we can develop an unthankful perspective that will affect the big answer, the answer on judgment day? Second Timothy 3:2 places "ungrateful" on a map to resisting the truth. After all, the truth is that God is good, that Christ is our Savior, and if we are ungrateful, we have already resisted the truth.

If we have grateful perspectives, our friends and those in our homes should know about it, and there's just no way they can find out about it if our dragons aren't involved. Jesus told the no-longer-demon-possessed man in Mark 5:19, "Go home to your friends and tell them how much the Lord has done for you, and how he has had mercy on you."

Are we telling? Those from my generation learned to count on *Sesame Street*. Each episode, in fact, was brought to us by a different number. *Sesame Street* never ever taught us to count silently in our head. Numbers were big, bold, and colorful.

When it comes to blessings, train your dragon to count out loud and in full color.

> But thanks be to God, who gives us the victory through our Lord Jesus Christ (1 Corinthians 15:57).

TRAINING POINTS

1. Today, if for a second you forget everything spiritual, what matters more than anything else in your immediate world? Keep this thought in your head. Now, consider your relationship

with Jesus Christ, your Lord and Savior. How does that other important thing truly compare with that relationship?

2. Do a little research on the evolution of Thanksgiving in our American culture. What is your favorite part about its history?

3. Read James 1:2–4. We need the entire passage to understand why we should count it as joy when we undergo trials. How can we see this principle in respect to our individual trials?

4. Have you ever been checked out by a cashier who could not do math? Share this experience as well as the frustration. How do you think God feels when we do the math wrong and come up with a focus on the negatives instead of His unspeakable gift?

THE TAIL END

And Speaking of Thanksgiving . . .

A centerpiece boasting the most colorful foliage of the season adorns the table atop a lace tablecloth. Autumn candles emit warm fragrances and highlight the kitchen masterpieces tempting impatient palates.

Also . . . there is a cookbook on fire on the stovetop, the brown 'n serve rolls have turned to black 'n serve, and there is a side of cranberry sauce which is shaped precisely like a can, including the rows of ridges in the middle of the column.

"It's 2:15!" people are randomly yelling from the den. "Are we going to eat any time before the next election? My blood sugar is dropping."

It's probably known most places as the finest feast of the year, Thanksgiving dinner, but we have had more than our share of challenges in pulling it off. There's just no easy way to defrost a turkey when you're down to six hours before the doorbell rings, and you're sticking the dough for the rolls in the dishwasher on the "hot air dry" cycle to see if it will rise fast enough. You're rationalizing with yourself, arguing that manmade traditions aren't so important, and after all, who doesn't like hot dogs?

What is it about Thanksgiving that makes us put things in our mouths we wouldn't dare think of the other 364 days? I'm not even sure I've ever even used the word *giblet* in a sentence, but suddenly the gravy has to have it. And pies are no longer about chocolate and caramel and tall meringue, but nutmeg and cinnamon. The salad has adopted something called Waldorf, and all the potatoes are sweet.

There's a lot to love about Thanksgiving. First of all, the very name itself implies that it is a time of giving thanks for the bountiful blessings we enjoy. Second, it is a time of family, and togetherness that, if just for the day, is a rare privilege to be cherished. These should be the themes of our gatherings, but if our special occasion was named each November, I fear it might receive the title, "Great Cooking Disasters of the Twenty-First Century."

Through the years, I have been known, at Thanksgiving or any other day, for creating new dishes, not really from scratch, but more like from "scratch your head and say, 'What is this?'" Here are a few of the culinary departments I've explored.

Interesting Texture

Store hours are not extremely convenient on holidays, so that when you find you're out of one of those peripheral pantry items such as, you know, flour or something like that, you desperately start searching the cookbook for cookie recipes that do not demand the key ingredient. I thought I had hit the jackpot when I found "Cornmeal Cookies" on page 49. The rest of the family was not so enthusiastic, but I convinced them saying, "It's in a national cookbook. How bad could it be?" That was the first mistake in my line of logic, but it got worse.

The mistake was not entirely my fault. I mean, who can really tell the difference between cornmeal and grits when they are poured in unlabeled containers? When my guests had earlier commented that they enjoyed trying things from *Southern Living*, they now added, "I didn't mean *that* Southern!"

Mystery Menu

The store had a cart with dinged up cans that were a fraction of the price of the ones on the shelves. Some of the cans were merely missing their labels, and one of these was a dime, so I thought I couldn't go wrong with that. I shook it enough to hear solids sloshing around in liquids and concluded it definitely wasn't pet food, and probably was a vegetable. It was a safe wager.

One night, I decided to have all of the elders and their wives over to get to know them after recently moving to the church. After the usual burning a couple of things, I resorted to scavenging for something, anything edible, which is where the mystery can came back into the equation.

Whatever it is, it will have to work—corn, beans, peas—I couldn't think of a vegetable I didn't like. That's because I couldn't think of beets. I have never even seen beets on a real table up until they were on mine. I know why the label was torn off now; it's the only way they could sell them. No one at the table had seen beets since they tasted them from a Gerber jar, and they obviously weren't about to change now.

Operator Error

I have had the greatest number of mishaps when trying to impress guests with homemade ice cream. One such guest was the president of a college, at which I demonstrated that my education at his fine institution was working out for me. Again, not entirely my fault that the ice cream recipe was not followed by the proper warning: *Hint: Put the paddle in before plugging in the freezer.*

Another ice cream episode involved hosting a dessert gathering for the small mission church where we encouraged all members to invite friends and family from the entire community. We wanted to make an impression. My ice cream did. I apparently sloshed it around enough in the bucket to get a great amount of salt from the ice surrounding the freezer into the actual ice cream itself. "Try mine, it's peach." I was strutting around like I was the next competition for Paula Deen. It was evoking comments like, "Mmmmm, yeah" and "This *is* peach. You want the rest of mine, honey?"

Not so for Andy, seven and honest as the day. His daddy scooped a hearty helping into his cup which he enthusiastically sipped through snaggleteeth, producing a sudden look of horror and a booming, "Mercy, Daddy! It's *mighty* bad!"

Our cooking adventures are a tradition, and they must also be genetic. My own dad's cutting edge kitchen experiments have included jelly-bean fried pies and thickening his Christmas candy with self-rising flour. My mom once simplified the au gratin potatoes by just using those pre-sliced cheese pieces you take out of the plastic wrapper. Only she forgot the "take out of the plastic wrapper" part.

And so as we turn the calendar to November, we envision juicy fat turkeys with moist dressing sitting beside heaps of cranberries in grandmother's antique bowl. We envision it that way, but deep inside we know the answer to the question which has puzzled so much of society:

"Why are there so many restaurants open on Thanksgiving these days?"

No one at the table had seen beets since they tasted them from a Gerber jar.

"From childhood you have known the holy scriptures."
—2 Timothy 3:15 NKJV

Train Your Dragon to
TEACH
Lead the Littlest Dragon in the Lair

Key Scriptures
Matthew 18:1–6; 19:13–30;
Mark 10:13–31; Luke 18:15–30

We had a beagle named Prissy. She did not know she was a beagle. She did not really think she was a breed of dog at all but was pretty sure she was a mix between a tabby grey and a calico cat. This was because when she was brought to the premises, it was already ruled by a couple of cats with Type A personalities. They were pretty annoyed that she showed up to infringe on their dynasty, but after walking around her a few times and sizing her up, they decided they would adopt her.

One of them in particular took on the project. He showed Prissy the ropes of how things worked around the place and who was in charge. Pretty soon, Prissy was pouncing on an untied shoe string, slapping at the cats when they got too near her, curling up on the warm hood of the car, and yawning like you were the most boring thing since algorithms. She had been led; she had been mentored; she had been trained. The academy was successful. The beagle graduated as a cat.

The Soul of a Child

One of the most powerful challenges our tongues can take on is to train, lead, mentor, and teach the youngest among us. We often fail to realize the paramount importance of a young soul. We can give the impression to children in our congregations that we're pretty annoyed they showed up to infringe on our dynasty.

We get pretty excited about them at showers and elaborate ceremonies revealing pink or blue. But then they arrive and we are hit with the reality that these beings are about a lot more than frilly bloomers and pastel pop-up books. And the excitement settles down somewhere just after the part about flushing the engagement ring and just before the part about spitting up on the judge.

Born with a maternal instinct, most of us have names picked out for our babies long before we know how they get here. But then after three or four of them are running around our den, we can't think of their names at gunpoint. The name of whoever it is we are trying to call down usually springs dead last from our lips, right after the dog. Or cat. Or whatever.

We read obituaries in which all of the adult relatives are named in full including first, last, middle, and maiden names, and the list tapers off by saying "and nine grandchildren."

I'm certainly not knocking the obituary form. I'm not even criticizing the fact that we usually forget our own children's names. But what we need to make absolutely sure of is that while we might forget a few details or succumb to a few formalities, we never forget the unarguable importance of the soul of a child. It's not that we need to start showing the child some attention one day as she nears the "age of accountability." It's that the formative years are now, her mind is able to absorb and retain truths like never again, and the relationships formed early are the ones that will be ingrained as the go-to places for strength and support.

An earlier chapter in this book is solely concerned with evangelism, urgent news for lost adults. I would not negate a word of its plea, but if there is an emphasis even more important than that, it's the urgency of teaching the children. Am I over the top on this? Is a little children's class equal in importance to a gospel meeting? That depends on how well you can swim. With a millstone around your neck.

Instruction from the Master Teacher

Jesus was not ambiguous about His stance on children. He says,

 But whoever causes one of these little ones who believe in me to sin, it would be better for him to have a great millstone fastened around his neck and to be drowned in the depth of the sea (Matthew 18:6).

- *Whoever.* If we back up to Matthew 18:1, we can see that Jesus' immediate listeners were the disciples of that time. But at the beginning of this warning, He clearly opens it up for you and me a couple of thousand years later with His use of "whoever." Some biblical communication was for Jews, some for Gentiles, some for first-century men and women, but without a doubt, when Jesus prefaces it with *whoever,* it's for me.

- *Causes.* The complete verb phrase is really "causes to sin." Other versions say "offends." We often use the word *offend* to mean hurt someone's feelings. We generally say, "I don't mean to offend you, but . . ." and what we're really saying is, "I'm about to blatantly hurt your feelings and somehow imagine I'm getting permission first and you won't care." That's not the flavor of meaning of *offend* in this passage. It really means to knock off track. Sin means to miss the mark, so we see the agreement between the translations. The thing is, it is very hard to get a train that has derailed back on the tracks, isn't it? Particularly without any damage or loss of lives. It makes more sense to be diligent in directing the train in the first place and being very watchful for any danger that might cause derailment.

Take heed. We can offend a child just by being negligent. When he begins to derail at about age thirteen or fourteen, we suddenly start blowing the whistle and pulling the alarms. We need a youth minister to help get this thing back on track. We need counseling. We need community service. We need something! I'm not negating any of those helps in crisis times, but how much easier it is to avoid the crisis altogether through constant awareness of the value of our dragons in teaching and training.

• *One.* We have to be concerned with each one. Each child we encounter is the most valuable one. The one who is cranky this morning. The one who smells like the cigarette smoke in his home. The one who was made to do her lesson, and the one who wasn't. The one who comes only on the Sundays when there is a meal or a game night. Those are the ones who need rescue the most. Hold on with every minute you've got. Have your dragon fill her mind with the teachings of Jesus when you can, because in this verse, she is one of the little ones.

And about that, I have heard some say that the phrase "little ones" here is not describing a child at all, but a baptized believer in Christ. Maybe it's true. I'm not a scholar in Greek or anything else, but I do know that when Jesus is saying "one of these little ones," there's a child in the middle of the circle, and it's one that He just placed there Himself. The fact that the child believes in Jesus does not mean that he understands everything about New Testament doctrine. Most three-year-old children can put us to shame with their simple faith in Jesus. I have heard more than one of them ask why we were crying at the passing of a loved one, telling us that being with Jesus after death would be the best thing that could ever happen. It makes you understand why robbing a child of this kind of faith is so evil. A few years ago, a children's home in Kentucky was told that houseparents could no longer pray with the orphaned or abandoned children who were placed there. How could you rob a child of the only Father he knows? Of the only hope in a hopeless world? It makes Jesus' next phrase even more sobering.

Each child we encounter is the most valuable one.

Millstone Necklace

> It would be better for him to have a great millstone fastened around his neck and to be drowned in the depth of the sea (Matthew 18:6).

Look at the choice of words.

• *Better.* Your chances are better at surviving such a scenario than of meeting Christ on judgment day after offending a child.

• *Great millstone.* My mom always told me to take my shoes off around water because if I were to fall in, the extra weight could keep me from swimming safely to shore. My husband, my dad, and some good friends of mine have all had to jump into water in an emergency with no time to kick off their shoes and have survived everything but humiliation, but a millstone would be a different story. Doing a little research, it looks like the average millstone weighs about three-fourths of a ton. But Jesus' millstone is not your average millstone. He calls His "a great millstone."

• *Neck.* And it's not attached to the feet either. I've had some heavy pendants before, but this takes plunder jewelry to a whole new level.

• *Depths.* Perhaps through some kind of Houdini amazement, someone could escape a water bath with a millstone around her neck, but not this one. This is the depths of the sea. The sea at its deepest is measured by miles and not by yardsticks.

Could the Lord have possibly used more alarming word pictures? Why are we not shaken over a lackadaisical attitude toward our youngest?

Important Interruption

Move over one chapter to Matthew 19. New chapter, same Savior. We are familiar with the text where Jesus beautifully takes the children into His arms (Matthew 19:13–14, Mark 10:16), but have we been careful to put the right frame around it?

In the immediate context, Jesus is having a crucial discussion with the Pharisees and disciples (Matthew 19:3–9). It's relevant, it's disturbing, and they are battling themselves to accept it. We're still there. It's brought up almost every time there is a Q & A lesson. What about divorce? What about second marriage?

And it's into this discussion that the people parade the little children. No wonder the disciples were prone to hold them at bay. You can almost hear them: "Oh no, not them. Not now."

Same?

Jesus was indignant at such a response from the disciples, according to Mark's account. We can allow Jesus to teach us rare truth and valuable doctrine, and at the same time cause Him to be indignant toward us because of our dismissal of children.

But when Jesus saw it, he was much displeased, and said unto them, "Suffer the little children to come unto me, and forbid them not: for of such is the kingdom of God" (Mark 10:14 KJV).

Much Displeased

Jesus was *much displeased* (KJV) when He saw the disciples' reaction. Is there significance to the word *much?* I think it's important if I'm in a cafeteria line and say, "I don't want much brussels sprouts, but I do want much mashed potatoes." I want the server to hear the word *much.*

Scripture says several times that the Lord is displeased with man's behavior.

- David's adultery with Bathsheba and his plotting of Uriah's death displeased God (2 Samuel 11:27).

- God was displeased with Onan, willing to receive sexual pleasure from Tamar, but unwilling to play the paternal role in providing an heir to his deceased brother—which was the whole point (Genesis 38:9–10).

- After God provided free and bottomless manna for a nation, Israel turned their nose up at it, loathed it, and longed to be back in bondage just so they could chomp an onion ring again. God was displeased (Numbers 11:1 NKJV).

But there is only one time I know of in scripture when God's displeasure is modified with the word *much*, and it is here in Mark 10:14. When the Lord saw the people turning away the children, He was *much* displeased.

Really? Does this indicate that a little shooing of children underfoot can upset God more than adultery, murder, sexual deviation, or longing for spiritual bondage? Here's the thing. What adulterer or murderer was not first a child? Did someone stand in the way of that child's learning, knowing, and loving Jesus before such a tragic future unfolded? From another angle, what elder or missionary was not first a child? Chances are, someone welcomed him into the arms of Jesus.

Prospects for Jesus

I could make a case for this, but no bother, because scripture already does in the very next verse in Mark's account. Jesus is surrounded by the children in Mark 10:16, and in the very next verse, "a man ran up and knelt before him and asked him, 'Good Teacher, what must I do to inherit eternal life?'" (Mark 10:17). We usually call him the rich young ruler. What a contrast to the children who came earlier. In our minds, which would we consider a better prospect? A child or this wealthy young adult? Several things come into play in our weighing scales.

When we encounter somewhat wealthy people, we are often drawn to them as a more promising prospect for the gospel than those who sputter into the parking lot in a car glued together with Bondo. In the gospel accounts we've examined, the children are penniless, but we call the young man rich because "he had great possessions" (Matthew 19:22).

He is also a ruler (Luke 18:18). Aren't we generally impressed with people of influence? I remember well when the town mayor came to one of our gospel meetings. Why do we not equally remember every other guest who walked through the door? By our faulty human standards, I'm afraid the children brought to Jesus would not have made it on our top ten list of prospects. After all, they were just kids.

And one of the most attractive things that made this rich man stand out as a great candidate for Christianity was his Bible knowledge. We're thrilled to get into Bible discussions quickly with those who have a background in scripture as this man did. In contrast, these children in the same chapter had experienced few years to accumulate this knowledge, so in a true sense, they were ignorant.

In addition to his knowledge, status, and wealth, this man came to Jesus with a solid reputation. Remember, his dragon spoke, "All these I have kept from my youth" (Matthew 19:20). We love to deal with the lost, as long as they're not real lost.

He was probably an upstanding man in the community, but what about the children? What were their reputations? Face it—a rowdy kid has a bad reputation. Everyone talks about his behavior. As for the compliant child, we wait to see what he will become. So at best, the children had unestablished reputations, and at worst, bad ones.

From every human standard, it appears that the rich young ruler outshined the children that day by a score that looked like the Alabama Crimson Tide was taking on the Assisted Living. It's a good thing that the souls that day weren't hinging on a human savior. It's a good thing that Jesus Christ, the Lord and Savior of all, was dealing directly with these people.

Most Promising Prospects

What made the real difference in these two accounts of how these people approached Jesus? The difference was that these children got to Jesus early, before the world had captured their hearts in material slavery. For the rich young ruler, it was just a little too late. Material possessions had a hold on him that he couldn't seem to shake.

Take it to heart. Try to reach every soul with the good news that will change his eternal destination, but never dismiss that the most promising prospect for receiving it is probably the one patting Bibles and coloring rainbows. The final result of the back-to-back stories is that the rich young ruler went away sorrowfully, but the little children entered Jesus' arms blessed.

Knowing this, I'd be careful about rolling my eyes in dread when approached by the deacon over education to teach the primary class. I think I'd be a little extra excited about putting stickers on the memory verse chart when I realize what's at stake.

And I think my dragon would sing out just a little louder "Jesus loves me" and "If the devil doesn't like it, he can sit on a tack!"

And he took a child and put him in the midst of them, and taking him in his arms, he said to them, "Whoever receives one such child in my name receives me, and whoever receives me, receives not me but him who sent me" (Mark 9:36–37).

Turned Away

A few years ago, a friend told me of an incident witnessed in his congregation. A young family had wanted to start a new chapter in life. They had little children, and the parents discussed and decided that they needed to be in church. It happened that our friend's congregation was nearby, and so not knowing one church from another, they checked it out. When the little girl nervously entered the new surroundings of her Bible class, the teacher counted her hand-outs and crafts. Then she counted heads and said to the little girl's mother, "I'm sorry. I don't have enough. She can't come to class today."

I wish it weren't a true story. Oh, how I wish it weren't true. For years, we also wished it weren't true that my dad's valuable watch slipped off one of our arms and fell into the river. We lamented it. It was a joyous occasion compared to the lament for a little soul who wanted to come to Jesus but was turned away. Now, in that light, I get the Savior's heartfelt displeasure at those disciples who tried to turn the children away.

But somebody brought those children to Jesus. They didn't come on their own. I like to think it was the mothers, but it's not always the mothers. Sometimes it's a grandmother; sometimes it's a Little League coach; sometimes a neighbor; and sometimes it's just an enthusiastic person who goes knocking on doors rounding kids up to get on a big old rowdy van. In every case, it takes a dragon.

Dragons, round up the children! Dragons, tell them about a God who loves them. Pray with them and sing out with the fervor that only a dragon tongue can carry, on key or not: Jesus loves the little children!

See that you do not despise one of these little ones. For I tell you that in heaven their angels always see the face of my Father who is in heaven (Matthew 18:10).

TRAINING POINTS

1. The same book of James that addresses our dragon problems also addresses our attitudes toward those who come into the assembly. How can we counter that initial reaction to distinguish those who come in with well-tailored mall clothing from those who sputter into the parking lot on bald tires and a duct-taped tarp for a window?

2. Make a list of ten children in your sphere of influence who need your spiritual direction. Of those ten, which three are most critically urgent? Think of one thing you can do for each of these three kids this week that will bond you closer. Next week, choose three more.

3. Notice this week in adult conversation what is said about children. Is it positive or negative? If it is negative, make a conscious effort to re-channel the conversation. What can we do to have a positive impact?

4. We can't miss the fact that the rich young ruler had obviously had some dragons training him, because he does mention that he had kept the commandments from childhood. Could it be that in the same way he was attached to material things, his teachers had also missed passing on the message of the danger of covetousness? It's a First-World problem. What are some specific ways to ensure that we get across to our children the importance of generosity, caring for the poor, and avoiding greediness that endangers our souls?

THE TAIL END

And Speaking of the Little Children's Class . . .

will never forget. She sat in a frilly Sunday dress, and with each shalt and shalt not, she wagged her head and her golden curls bounced in rhythm. "Remember the Sabbath day to keep it holy; Honor thy father and thy mother; Thou shalt not kill." It was then that I knew our weeks of study, take-home reminders, and visual reinforcements had paid off, and as the teacher, I was feeling a tinge of pride, but then she said it. "Thou shalt not admit adultery."

Somewhere just between attendance chart stickers and coloring sheets, she had missed the point. But she nailed the conviction of a lot of adults.

How is it that as Bible class teachers, we can become so enthused about communicating a concept to our class in a fun and innovative way, and in two seconds they can totally train-wreck an hour and forty-five minutes' worth of preparation time? I remember wanting to emphasize hospitality in a lesson about Lydia, so I brought a pineapple. "Does anyone know what this symbolizes?" I did that slow, circular teacher strut as I held it up high.

A little boy held his hand just as high, and said, "I do!" followed by, "It's SpongeBob's house, isn't it?"

The deal is, even when my plans get railroaded, I love to teach. It's hard for me to comprehend the deacon's having to bribe and beg people to give up an hour a week to spend with young eager souls thirsting for the Word.

Many years ago, one such deacon came up to my mom after services and, while I'm pretty sure his thought was *I need a teacher in the worst way*, what came out of his mouth was, "I need a teacher of the worst kind." I guess she should have been offended, but after the initial amusement, she said, "Well, you've come to the right place."

I visited a congregation when my four children were small. The greeter was delighted with our presence as she began to drop the children off in the appropriate rooms. But the teacher? Not so much. As the greeter smiled, "And this is Enoch; he'll be in your class tonight," the teacher took one look at him and said, "Will you get me some help?" I guess he had that effect. We visited another congregation, and this time when I entered the classroom with him, the teacher was thrilled to see us. In fact, she said, "I'm so glad you're here," but then the reason became evident. "Will you teach my class?"

Maybe teachers experience burnout, maybe they're encountering personal hurdles, but I hear more and more that teachers are afraid they will be unsuccessful at classroom management. Classroom management is really not an issue for me. I can manage the classroom with ease. It's when the kids begin to show up in it that the trouble starts.

Whatever the reason for our hesitancy to teach, and

> The teacher took one look at him and said, "Will you get me some help?"

it's probably more Satan in one of his shrouds than anything else, we must dismiss it in favor of the urgency of Bible knowledge.

Without the teaching program in place, how will young lives be impacted by good Samaritan kindness, how will they know the true happiness found in the beatitudes, and how will they ever understand the unique identity of God's people, His church? But with the teaching program in place, how will we ever clean up this monstrosity of a place we call the teachers' workroom?

Granted, it's hard to spend so much time illustrating the Babylonian captivity that you feel like you've been in it, and then use the drawing for thirty minutes before throwing it away. I understand the mindset of saving materials for possible later use. But it kind of gets out of hand when we have confetti from 1972, and a flip chart of children named things that our grandmothers are named wearing post-colonial clothing that we're not sure is supposed to be orange or red because of sun fading, and we'll never find out by asking the original teacher because it's kind of difficult to answer questions posthumously. Giant bulletin board cut-outs are luminously bowing over filing cabinets, so that if we did ever really put them in use again, the bulletin board would have to communicate the message of osteoporosis prevention. I have a project for the space team. Quit worrying about whether conditions are suitable for life on Mars. Check out its capacity for storage.

And then . . . And *then* . . . with all this stash of generations of materials, should you need something completely mundane such as dry erase markers, not a soul in the congregation can come up with one at gunpoint. This Sunday I marched my class down to the next room because mine was missing the markers. Though there was a recently colored-on board there, the markers had evacuated. We then unlocked a few doors before going to the teen class, asking them, and meeting with blank stares. I then scribbled a note to the teacher of the auditorium class, delivered it, and bingo. In the middle of a discussion of Job's three friends, he interjected, "Office desk, left side, third drawer," and then moved on to verse 14.

I don't know about your teaching style, but I have to employ a variety of methods to drive home the point. We read aloud, we glue macaroni, we dry erase, and we sing.

While we have a set repertoire of children's songs in class, I'll admit I've deferred to singing a few of these more familiar songbook ones to console myself after the final bell:

- After dealing with a particularly spoiled child, "This class is not his home; he's just a-passing through."

- After realizing that eighteen five-year-olds cannot use scissors, "Take time to be cutting-out pieces ahead of time."

- After painting walls, hanging curtains, and mounting posters, "I shall not be; I shall not be moved!"

- After the custodian has straightened the classroom, "He took my pencils all away."

- After forty-five minutes in the toddler class, "Let all the earth keep silence before me."

- After an assistant shows up fifteen minutes late, "She is able to deliver me."

- And at 8:01 PM every Wednesday, with a sigh of relief, "Now the day is over."

If you have not yet joined the adventure of teaching, you should give it some thought. It won't kill you, although there are days when I think we should all get a memo: You're signed up to teach. Bring your Bible . . . and emergency contacts . . . and a will.

(Originally printed in *Christian Woman* magazine, S/O 2016)

Train Your Dragon to STAND

Learn Boldness on the Hot Seat

Key Scriptures
James 3:10; Galatians 2:13; Luke 22:55–60;
Hebrews 10:25; Acts 2:46

Why do they do this? It's part of the dog code. Apparently, the labradoodle sets his alarm for 3:15 AM every day for the ritual and starts barking hysterically as if the entire second floor of an Angola prison dorm has escaped and is headed straight for his dinner bowl. This causes an unfightable urge in a Yorkie a block away to start saying the same thing. Pretty soon there is a symphony of highly annoying minor chords closing down any hope you have of a good night's sleep. There is no cause. There is no boogeyman loose. There is no trace of even a threatening mosquito. You know, because you have gone outside more than once in your lifetime in nothing but a T-shirt and a blanket carrying a flashlight and a baseball bat. The barking escalates as if to say, "We are not making this up. Ask my brother; he saw the whole thing."

The truth is, it's a giant hoax. The only reason that any dog except the first one is

barking is simply because each dog wanted to do what every other dog is doing and say what every other dog is saying.

It seems a pointless rationale, but our dragons also have a high propensity for joining in for no other reason than . . . well . . . joining in.

It reminds me of an *I Love Lucy* episode where Lucy orders what she wants from the menu, but then when Ricky orders, she changes her mind to what he's having, until Ethel orders, and then she changes her mind again. Whatever is being said around her sounds good to her.

Christian Code or World Code?

Our language, as Christians, ought to be different from the language of those around us. James says so: "Out of the same mouth proceed blessing and cursing. My brethren, these things ought not to be so" (James 3:10). But it is exactly what happens sometimes. I read the following on a social media site the other day: "God puts people in your life for a season and for a reason." This was sandwiched between two other posts by the same person on the same social media wall, both of which were brimming with multiple curse words.

It may be that we would never let such foul comments come out of our mouths or be on our walls, but there is somehow a temptation to prove that we can come as close as possible without crossing the line. Those who know me best know that I love humor maybe a little more than I should. I'd rather laugh than eat. But just barely. But there's really nothing funny in crass words, innuendo, abrasive slurs, and really close euphemisms. Just because the woman in the desk next to us does it, doesn't mean a Christian should have whatever she's having. Coarse speech is not attractive. It does draw attention if that's what you want, but so do busted zippers and mustard on your chin.

No human being can tame the tongue. It is a restless evil, full of deadly poison. With it we bless our Lord and Father, and with it we curse people who are made in the likeness of God (James 3:8-9).

Whatever She's Having

But the "having whatever you're having" problem goes beyond this. Sometimes we find ourselves in full verbal agreement with that which, at best, is a tug away from Christian morals and scriptural mandates. It seems if we are around it enough, our mouths shift to automatic and start sounding like the one in the office chair next to us—whatever she's having. I can't think of any other reason for this kind of shift. There are friends who used to sit up all night with me in college because our consciences were giving our tongues a workout. We talked about everything from near misses in church attendance to near concerts in worship formats. We thumbed through concordances like they were the last issue of *Rolling Stone* trying to find if a teaching was what Jesus said or just what somebody said the preacher said the Bible said.

I would have bet a king-size Butterfinger, if I were a betting woman, that none of those dragons would ever leave the lair, but I might lose the bet. How is it that those same friends now send me messages telling me they've joined a church recently that isn't quite the one we read about in the New Testament? How is it that their social media profiles have something other than Christian for religion? How is it that that they're verbal activists for *not* defining marriage as between a man and woman? How have we come this far from the soul searching in those days? I really don't think you can get here from there without a whole lot of foolish speaking in between—without a whole lot of dragons ordering exactly like Lucy did.

Does our dragon just say, "I'll have whatever she's having"? Speech that compromises; speech that yields to the crowd, speech that yields to pressure. It can happen within the church-building walls, and it can happen out in the world. It happened in Galatians 2:13 when it says that even Barnabas was carried away with the hypocrisy of those around him.

Even Barnabas was carried away with the hypocrisy of those around him.

It happened in Luke 22 when Peter's mouth felt extreme pressure to deny what he knew to be true, and to curse.

> Then he began to invoke a curse on himself and to swear, "I do not know the man." And immediately the rooster crowed (Matthew 26:74).

Denial of the living God is foolish speaking, and we can deny knowing Him directly as Peter did, or we can deny Him by trying to sound agreeable and conforming to the world's patterns. At the office, at the gym, at the play day, we can nod along with talk that supports immoral trends—murder labeled as pro-choice, adultery labeled as marriage, drunkenness labeled as good times, and lust labeled as prom night. Dragons next to us favor movies, shows, and songs that are at the top of the charts, but which really promote everything that Christ's blood is trying to save us *from!* And then when we are put on the spot, we find our own dragons, maybe to our surprise at first, forming some words that fall in line with exactly what the crowd is saying. I remember watching a talk show during election season in which politicians were put on the spot to answer whether they believed in evolution or not. Some said that they did, some hemmed and hawed, and only two of the eight or so in the room confidently affirmed the literal six-day creation in scripture.

Closer to home, some years ago a call-in show featured as its guests several religious leaders, diverse in their doctrines, but Christian in their claims. A caller asked their views on Islam. The climate was such that pluralism—many approaches to God—was being embraced and almost enforced, particularly by one on the panel. Another panelist, at one time a faithful gospel preacher in the Lord's church, was asked to comment on the caller's question. Here's what the preacher said, "Well, I guess it depends on if he's asking it from a political or religious point of view." The moderator clarified that it was religious, to which he responded, "Religious point of view—it is a different approach to God than the Christian approach to God. My understanding as a Christian is that we're saved by what Christ did for us, whereas the Islamic faith [sic] we're saved by what we do for God. So you've got two different angles, two different approaches to God" (CNN).

On Guard, Dragon

In a moment when Christ could have been lifted up before hundreds of thousands as the Way, the Truth, and the Life, it became, instead, an "I'll have whatever you're having" moment. The statement succumbed to the pressure of the crowd. Guard against it at all costs. Here are four ways:

1. *Stay in the Word.* Keep a comprehensive knowledge of the Bible through regular study, so that you never really have to say what you think but can always defer to the Holy Spirit. "Have whatever *He's* having."

2. *Keep an open conversation going with your Father.* At regular times? Yes. Every morning? Good. But also as opportunities present themselves around you, ask for help to get it right before you open your mouth.

3. *Keep company as much as you can with Christians,* as Hebrews 10:25 says, "Not neglecting to meet together," and Acts 2:46 says, "Day by day attending the temple together and breaking bread in their homes." When we're living our lives as one family of God, that support carries over into confidence in the face of the enemy and in the midst of the crowd.

4. *Realize and accept up front that you're going to be ridiculed.* You don't have to win every argument, or even have the first one, to stand successfully. God's wisdom is foolishness to the world (1 Corinthians 1:18 NKJV). If they think you're strange, it's a good sign (1 Peter 4:4 NKJV).

Don't let your dragon fall in line with whatever everyone else is having, when all that really matters is what He orders.

For we have spent enough of our past lifetime in doing the will of the Gentiles—when we walked in lewdness, lusts, drunkenness, revelries, drinking parties, and abominable idolatries. In regard to these, they think it strange that you do not run with them in the same flood of dissipation, speaking evil of you. They will give an account to Him who is ready to judge the living and the dead (1 Peter 4:3–5 NKJV).

TRAINING POINTS

1. Watch a few morning-show interviews this week. Keep a tally of how many times the voice of the crowd is opposed to what God's word teaches. Write a scripture down each day beside those tally marks that will keep your dragon careful to speak the truth and not chime in with the masses.

2. Every time you are in the car alone this week, talk to God on the way to where you're going, and ask Him for wisdom to say the right thing in a conversation when you get there—something that will bring someone closer to Him and His truth.

3. If you are belittled this week for your "backward" aversion to sin, start a habit of immediately thanking God that your dragon had the opportunity to stand, and rejoice that you were counted worthy (Acts 5:41).

4. How do we respond to the popular admonition to "coexist" with other religions? How do we accept the fact that "little g" gods permeate our culture without accepting that our friends, colleagues, and families are destined to serve them and be lost to them?

5. Go to a large secular bookstore and pick up five colorful children's books in the science section. How many of these, somewhere near the beginning, talk about the origins of the planets or the animals or whatever is being featured in the book? Write a sentence down from one of these. Then when you get home, make a list of scientific reasons that one sentence cannot be true. Sometimes, when we examine just one sentence of the rhetoric we are buying into, we realize that our dragons do not have to nod along.

6. Invite a college student to lunch this week. She is going through a natural phase of examining her beliefs and solidifying her faith as she forges independence. Give her a bond that will support her through the challenges. Text her verses twice a week with comments such as, "This made me think of you," "This made me smile," "I hope this impacts your day the way it did mine," or "This is why I love you."

7. Think of a pretty way to display the words of John 14:6 in a prominent place. Treasure it every day as a reminder for your dragon to stand.

8. Sometimes our dragons use their fingertips as much as their tongues as we type words for all the world to see on social media. What are some practical guidelines we should follow so that the world notices our stand without being annoyed with our rants?

9. Instead of looking for negative posts this week on social media, look for Christian dragons that are standing up for God and take a second to comment, "I appreciate you."

THE TAIL END

And Speaking of Setting an Alarm . . .

Why does everyone's work except for mine? I can set an alarm for something extremely important, such as the first one hundred customers get a honeybun, and I can check it two or three times before I go to bed to make sure it's set, and in the morning nothing happens. The Quick Mart has been open for three hours, there are people walking underneath my window eating free honeybuns, and my alarm is sitting in dead silence as if to whisper, "Gotcha!"

There's always a reason it didn't go off. I had it on silent, I set it for PM instead of AM, I was in a different time zone, my phone died in the middle of the night, the power went off, or wait—was daylight saving's time today? Even though my alarm pretty consistently fails me, I find that I am the only person in the universe who has this problem. When I go to a retreat or camp or just decide that I'm going to sleep in the next morning after an exhausting night, I find that everyone else's alarms work perfectly fine.

And I find out that people get up at indecent hours to do things like jog in the moonlight, watch the Royal Wedding in the middle of the night, set the ham out to thaw, or go take the ACT test on a Saturday. Can't they start those at noon? Or get this—I was a camp counselor, spelled C-O-U-N-S—D-E-A-D-T-I-R-E-D, and two teenage girls set their alarms for 3:30 AM to . . . wash their HAIR!!!

I stumbled out of the bunk and said, "Whasoo doin' sup oh early?"

"Oh, we're going to wash our hair," with a completely normal expression as if they had just said they were going to do something mundane like roll another cabin or whatever.

"Wash your hair?? At 3:00 AM??? At CAMP??? We forget to even wash our hair all week."

"Yeah, you're right," they say. "Let's wait until 3:10," nodding in agreement and falling back into the bunk.

This is where I learned a very important thing about life. I. Hate. Snooze buttons.

I try to love everyone, but those people who push the little snooze button so it goes off again every seven minutes, and it does this about as many times as a Kennedy has been in office—those people test my limits.

I remember saying to the girls in the cabin, "Look, I think you've mistaken this term *counselor*. You see, I don't have any kind of psychology degree or clinical license. Anyone who sets an alarm for 3:00 AM who is not having surgery at 3:45 needs a kind of help I'm unqualified to give."

And I mean, these occasions that warrant waking your roommate up would not be so bad if everyone just had a regular beep or ding-a-ding alarm clock. But I find myself startled by, "To the batcave! Hurry, Batman, or Gotham City will be destroyed forever!"

And I answer, "That's not the only thing that's about to be destroyed forever. It's ridiculous-thirty in the morning, Batman. Take a sedative."

No, I'm not crazy about alarm clocks, but apparently other people think they're great fun. One of the favorite pranks in college was to sneak in and change someone's clock time and alarm, so that they would think they were getting up at, oh, 7:30 when in reality it was 2:00 AM, which happened to be

People get up at indecent hours to do things like jog in the moonlight.

146 • How to Train Your DRAGON

my prime time for studying out in the hall so as not to wake up my roommate.

I was in just such a hall with my sociology book, a notebook, and a picnic lunch, when this cute girl, a victim of the alarm clock prank, comes bouncing down the hall with her backpack in tow and her hair freshly curled. "Hi, Beth," I said.

She stopped dead still because I think she could tell I was in late-night-cramming mode and not morning-running-late-frenzy mode, and she didn't say hi back. She could only say, "What time is it?" I broke the news, and she still didn't say hi. In fact, she did an about-face, and went marching with a fury saying, "Who did this to meeeeeeeee?!"

I get it. I completely understand the frustration. My husband sets the alarm for 6:50 every morning. I don't care if it's Christmas Day; that thing goes off. And it's a radio one, so I'm sandwiched between two men: one man who is unfazed by any noise and is snoring the entirety of Mozart's 41st symphony, and one man who is talking non-stop about the weather, the traffic jam on I-565, and one morning he said that I could win a hundred dollars if I could be the first caller and my birthday was November (pause) the (pause) fifth. Match! I went from groggy to greedy in 2.5, frantically searched for my phone, stubbed my toe, and screamed all of the notes of the symphony that he had not yet snored.

Yeah, I hate alarm clocks. It's nothing new. The rooster was the most hated animal in the Garden of Eden. I don't have book, chapter, and verse, but I'm pretty sure Eve came bouncing through the trees with a fury in her eyes, asking every bird in the henhouse . . .

"Who did this to meeeee?!"

Train Your Dragon to SING

Embrace the Gift That Gets Us Through

Key Scriptures

Exodus 15:2; Acts 16:25; 1 Corinthians 14:15;
Colossians 3:16; John 4:24

Morning dragons are not among the best. Some dragons don't operate at all until after the first cup of coffee. But some do. Some get up disheveled and half blind. They kick off the covers and reach for their contacts. Let's hope no one left thumb tacks on the nightstand because anything close will do as they take a sip from the flower vase. These dragons utter nonsensical things such as, "Who took my sunshay mmoostop?" Don't laugh because this may nudge them into a little clarity, they will realize you are there, and you will suddenly be responsible for everything awry in the pre-shower phase of their almost reality.

Then there is a third classification of morning dragons. These dragons wake up with a song bursting past their morning breath, and it is never a break-up song or a funeral march. It's a motivational speech put to music as they do jumping jacks on the way to the toilet. These are among the most hated dragons, but that doesn't faze them at all. They couldn't care less what you think of their cheerful energy. It's a new day, and they won't even remember the law of entropy exists until at least 1:00 PM when it hits like a pop-up storm at a tee-ball game.

Our feathered friends are the same. You've got these unholy roosters that wake up at ridiculous-thirty AM for no other reason than to say, "Hey everyone, I've got a scratchy voice that people can hear for miles, and I can hold the last note longer than Celine Dion without gargling first." Unfortunately, these guys wake up the crows who hold a popular gossip session that sounds like it's inches from your bedroom window.

But then there are the singers. Just when you were thinking about getting up and loading a shotgun that you don't even own, the morning singers bring peaceful and soothing notes. It turns out that the smallest birds carry the most talented voice boxes, and as they blend with one another in a short chorus, they convince you that you can put both feet on the floor one more time.

I will sing to the Lord, because he has dealt bountifully with me (Psalm 13:6).

From Crying to Singing

One of the greatest blessings common to all of humanity is that we share the little bird's gift. Each baby is born with pretty strong vocal chords, and before he can get all the way out of the womb and even ask what's for lunch, he shows them off with a cry. But it isn't many months into life that the little one learns that these same vocal chords can manage a range of notes, and the lifetime gift of humming occurs. Pretty soon, words that sound like the Greek alphabet attach themselves to the notes, and if you could get him to draw a scale and train his hand to place the notes in the right shapes and on the right lines, you'd have a Tchaikovsky on your hands.

Don't let the tendency to sing yourself through any situation that you don't cry through fade away with childhood. By the way, there are some pretty valuable songs we teach our littles that usually don't make it from the cradle roll to the auditorium, but why not? Simple truths are among the most profound. Think about the value of the messages in these lyrics from children's songs:

- *I love to pat the Bible; it tells me of God.*
- *Red and yellow, black and white; they are precious in His sight.*
- *If you're happy and you know it, then you really ought to show it.*
- *Roll the gospel chariot along.*
- *All around the neighborhood; I'm gonna let it shine.*
- *It isn't any trouble just to p-r-a-y, pray.*
- *If the devil doesn't like it, he can sit on a tack!*

What if each adult carried the main thought from each one of those lyrics with her every day? The result would be: *Bring it on; I'm ready!*

I'm thankful that those lyrics were put in my head before I could count to twenty or tie my shoes. But I'm also thankful for the "big girl" ones that have come along since. How many times was I ready to throw my hands up and cry like a newborn, but then some words came to my mind and spilled out of my dragon that directed my paths toward perspective.

- *Kneel at the cross; Christ will meet you there.*
- *How deep the Father's love for us; how vast beyond all measure.*
- *My sin—oh, the bliss of this glorious thought. My sin—not in part, but the whole—is nailed to the cross, and I bear it no more. Praise the Lord. Praise the Lord! Oh, my soul.*

Those lyrics were put in my head before I could count to twenty or tie my shoes.

- *Eager eyes are watching, longing, for the lights along the shore.*
- *Lead me gently home, Father.*
- *Ask the Savior to help you; comfort, strengthen, and keep you.*

Singing Heritage

Our dragons have a singing heritage. The first thought that occurred to the Israelites after God had ushered them through the Red Sea and caused the great walls of water to collapse on Pharaoh, was a song. And among the first lyrics of it were,

 The Lord is my strength and my song (Exodus 15:2).

A few thousand years later, we too have been delivered from bondage. We turn our head to see the failure of our pursuer. Around us there are some pretty vile songs riding the radio waves, but none of those are our song. We don't have to listen or sing those tunes. The *Lord* is our strength and song.

At midnight, bruised and bloody, Paul and Silas sang (Acts 16:25). At midnight, those of us who are hurting and know the lyrics best, also sing. Our dragon does it for us. When circumstances seem so bleak, when our heart is crushed and we can't seem to turn it just right to get it to fit into place again, when our friends have become our foes and our foes have become a pestilence, our heart tries to cry out to our Salvation, but the words trip on one another on an unstable course. We haven't yet found the arm-strength to reach for the Bible on the nightstand. That will come, but in the meantime, the dragon takes over. In spiritual ICU quarters, the singing dragon stands watch and feeds us the words. And we remember them. "His grace reaches me." "My Jesus knows." "He will pilot me." Like an unseen IV pumping fluids we can't swallow, the words of familiar songs rush through our veins giving us the adrenaline needed to resolve to recover.

> Now therefore write this song and teach it to the people of Israel. Put it in their mouths, that this song may be a witness for me against the people of Israel (Deuteronomy 31:19).

Singing Sticks to the Brain

What is it about a song that can rouse our dragons to life when the status is code blue? God designed us that way. He knows all about it, but scientists are still trying to figure it out. They are learning that song lyrics are stored in a specific lobe of the brain, and that may be why they come to us more readily than that of other knowledge we have learned. This may be true of songs heard over and over on the radio, electronic devices, and home speakers, but there is another level of memory that makes solid gold hits on the Christian minds.

Those tasks that we learn as we do them, motor skills, stay with us in a permanent way. It's exactly why we say, "It's like riding a bicycle" about something we just don't forget. See, the act of listening to lyrics put to music uses some pretty good ink as it writes on the brain. But if you want to remove song memory from those who have participated in singing on a regular basis, and particularly from a young age, get a putty knife and elbow grease. And good luck! It's not happening.

Maybe you have worshiped at a nursing home, and the range of cognizance in the room is from full to none. Some could probably handle the conducting end better than we do, but some do not know why they are there, and a few don't even know who they are. But something happens when the singing begins. Weak voices get a little stronger as they can remember in automatic every single word and note. Christians have a very special gift that turns into a most valuable resource. Sing with one

In spiritual ICU, the singing dragon stands watch and feeds us the words.

another every chance you have. Sing praise. Sing thanks. Sing stamina. Sing scripture.

And never rob the very young of having beautiful scores of wisdom permanently engraved in their minds this way. Oh, they might not get the full meaning at the time. When my nephew Abel was four, his mother went through a busy time cleaning out and redoing her house amid other responsibilities. I think Abel had added a word to his vocabulary during the week, and it came out loud and clear as he sang "His glory is exhausted!" in worship Sunday where the bats in the belfry could hear.

When my sister Cindy was little, she understood "Sweetly the tones are falling" to be "Sweet little plums are falling," which would explain the "open the door for me." Another of my friends misread "There's a stranger at the door" to be "There's a strangler at the door," which would *not* explain the "let him in" part. We all have our favorite misread or misquoted lyrics from the smallest of interpreters including, "The morning of George," "Up from the grave he arose with a mighty star upon his nose," and the child who asked a VBS song leader I know, right after they had sung the books of the New Testament, "Why *did* he bruise James?"

Embrace the sincere mistakes. They show the greater blessing that before the truth of the songs are even comprehended by the child, they are forging their way into the crevices of his mind and will equip him with words that will manhandle the trials and sorrows when he can't.

A Song Says It All

During the waning days of 2017, I gathered with my family around my daddy's bed. He was a singer and a whistler and a hummer. He filled in gaps with his own silly lyrics and did a little creative maneuvering of the melodies as well. Two weeks earlier, he had gotten out of bed to get dressed to go sing and worship with his Christian family, as he had done almost every Sunday for ninety-five years. But what a difference two weeks make. Now his lungs were giving up on him. As one of us would say "I love you, Daddy," he would slowly frame "I love" but couldn't finish. What could we do but look at one another and pray inside? We had done everything we could do: turned him, lifted him, laid him back down, talked to him, showed him pictures, run for the nurse, and cried out to the Maker of makers.

It wasn't hard to know what to do then, because we have a heritage. The Lord is my strength and my song. A few days earlier, as I was alone with Dad, he had become preoccupied with the words of the song, "I Am the Vine." He kept asking me if I could get someone to sing it. And now here we were together with him. So we sang. We sang not only that song, but other favorites as well until gratitude replaced despair, truth dispelled doubt, and joy conquered worry.

No one ran their finger over the notes to see if we were observing the fermata or if the flat note was flatter than it was supposed to be. It was the words that fortified us, but as our dragons put the melody with it and blended in some harmony, it cemented the moment; the relationships; and the confidence in our Shepherd, Shield, and Savior. Only a song can do it in that way.

 Behold, God is my salvation; I will trust, and will not be afraid; for the Lord God is my strength and my song, and he has become my salvation (Isaiah 12:2).

Give the Half-Note a Rest!

There is a little mosquito that can plague even a big dragon, though. Its name is Form-Over-Function, but it's not found in the "singing" passages of scripture.

- First Corinthians 14:15 says, "I will sing praise with my spirit, but I will sing with my mind also."

- Colossians 3:16 says, "Let the word of Christ dwell in you richly, teaching and admonishing one another in all wisdom, singing psalms and hymns and spiritual songs, with thankfulness in your hearts to God."

- And John 4:24 says, "God is spirit, and those who worship him must worship in spirit and truth."

We have multiple commands that our songs should be spirit-driven, full of meaning, and faithful to the truth. I'm thankful that we have no commands that our voices should be stellar in excellence and training, and that our adherence to musical notation should be painstakingly careful.

I'm all for doing it right. I admire those who have the ability to distinguish nuances of change in the notation. But truth be told, there's not a verse of scripture about it. Do your best. We all feel better when we sound better. But be careful. We can overlook a treasure while looking over a measure. I remember times of sitting in front of a brother or sister who belted out praise with a monotone dragon, and I was still admonished, maybe even more so because of the reminder of singing with the spirit.

If you want to teach music fundamentals to our singers and you have the know-how, go for it! We need you. But don't ever be caught griping about a musical mistake, inability, or just opinion of how it should be done. Instead, focus on the glorification of God and the spirit of brotherhood that accompanies the joyful noise. I attended an area-wide event a few years ago, and there was a large number of teens there. The singing was tremendous. I think a few tears tried to well up as I heard them sing about the Father's love, redemption, and resolve. There was spirit. There was understanding. There was joy. It kept me going for a few days, and I sang along with my memories of that night. It had happened on a Sunday night.

On Tuesday of that same week, a sister made a comment within a small group, and she was displeased that the notes to all the songs were not projected with the lyrics. Someone else said that the songs were new and they didn't know all of them, and after several other criticisms were voiced, the summation was that these young people were just trying to show out by singing so enthusiastically.

The Form-Over-Function mosquito buzzed around that room and it was

We can over-look a treasure while looking over a measure.

heartbreaking, discouraging, and just plain wrong. Our function is to praise God and build one another up. That Tuesday conversation reminded me of something that happened in Job 1:6, "Now there was a day when the sons of God came to present themselves before the Lord, and Satan also came among them." When our family of God presents their voices before the Lord in spirit, truth, and understanding, that other guy wants in. Don't let him.

Let us continually offer up a sacrifice of praise to God, that is, the fruit of lips that acknowledge his name (Hebrews 13:15).

Lyrics for Happy Dragons

In this house, we're familiar with the handed-down hymns that get us through not only church assembly days but all the other ones as well. They're not reserved for just devotional periods, but string along with us through the most harried and chaotic moments of our day-to-day. We all know that the answer to "scoot over, you're about to knock me off" is: *Where could I go but to the Lord?* When little people (or big people) complain about a chore, they know they're about to hear, *Tempted and tried, we're oft made to wonder why it should be thus all the day long.* If the couch is too crowded, we're told to go sit: *Over there, over there, over there, over there, you'll soon be at home over there.* When someone is almost finished with a term paper, *what a day of rejoicing that will be!* After a retelling of a fender bender, we hear, *Did you sue for loving favor?* When the driver isn't proceeding on a green light, he gets, *Why do you wait, dear brother?* But mostly, when dessert is making its way around the table . . . *Do not pass me by.*

The Lord is my strength and my shield; in him my heart trusts, and I am helped; my heart exults, and with my song I give thanks to him (Psalm 28:7).

TRAINING POINTS

1. What children's song has the most enduring and important message to you?

2. What hymn is your favorite and why? Which lyric line in it is the most valuable to you?

3. Read an article on the web this week about music and memory. Share your findings with others in your class. How does this enhance your view of your Creator? Thank Him for it.

4. Share some lyrics that you misheard as a child, or that a child you know misheard.

5. First Corinthians 14:15; Colossians 3:16; and John 4:24 are mentioned in this chapter. What other verses about singing emphasize our heart over our vocal accuracy?

6. Have you been taught by singing in assembly? Have you been encouraged? How does this work?

THE TAIL END

And Speaking of Jumping Jacks . . .

They're not as much fun as they used to be, are they? I'm pretty sure the Jack that was jumping when we were kids is dead by now. How is it that P. E. used to be our favorite class of the day, and when the bell rang to go back to history class, we'd beg for one more lap around the track? Now we're begging, pleading for one less lap, and we'd exchange it for a weeklong lecture on the Ming dynasty.

And we thought sweat was a bad thing back then. Our fifth-grade teacher would double check with everyone to make sure they had administered deodorant in the proper fashion and the proper place. No one wanted to be caught sweating when a cute guy walked by.

Now the cute guys and girls are the ones promoting sweat. We're actually paying money to "Sweat with Kaitlyn." One website said sweat is a badge of honor. Wait, I studied my heart out trying to get a spelling medal, and all I had to do was just sweat?

Let's examine a few ways to strive for this badge of honor.

Invest in the Big Equipment

Suddenly, we're coerced to buy exercise equipment on the promise that if we will exercise fourteen minutes, we can drop six dress sizes in eight weeks. The thing is, I'm not seeing any of these exercise models wearing dresses. They didn't lose dress sizes; they lost the whole dress.

They're pretty much wearing just slightly more than I wore at my last mammogram and get this, even though the equipment is sold with the incentive that you can exercise in the comfort—comfort is a word meaning sweating like a pig and panting like a dog while you grit your teeth like Rocky—of your own home, in the ad

I'm seeing, the girl is working out on this machine against a background of clouds and skyscrapers. Where does she live? In the middle of the smokestacks on top of a high-rise? And if so, who delivered that two-ton gadget up there?

And how will she ever get down? These bicycles are rigged so that the person can pedal and pedal, and the thing doesn't move an inch. What kind of rip-off is that?

Workout to a Video with No Equipment Needed

If we're honest with our bodies, we really don't need equipment that will affect our family's credit rating for generations to come. There are plenty of exercises we can do with no equipment at all. I hate 'em. But I do them, especially when I can't think of an excuse not to.

After all, there are a lot of realities that can drive us. Exercise releases endorphins, helps with weight loss, strengthens our muscles and bones, but none of these thoughts are driving me when I get ten minutes into the routine. Only one thought helps me through: There will be no leg lifts in heaven. Which makes me wonder, by the way, why am I trying to delay that transition?

In constantly trying to find a way to make misery fun, we succumb to watching the energetic guy on the video. He makes it look so easy, calling it the total body workout. Before trying it, I struggled with knowing what was "the sin unto death."

Now I think I may know. I'm wondering what kind of workout I could get for, say, thirty percent of the body.

"There is nothing new under the sun." Solomon said it. It's true of fashion, it's true of food, and it's true of exercise. We just call them new things. Like

Only one thought helps me through: There will be no leg lifts in heaven.

kettlebell swings, air squats, and burpees. It kind of sounds like every discussion I find myself surrounded by since the girls went away to college and I live in a male household. Just throw an explosion or two in there and you've got dinner conversation. You can call it what you want, but the truth is still the truth. Healthy workouts are killing me!

But the music is nice. Nothing like a soundtrack of "Shake your body down to the ground" to get you going. I got through that okay, but do you have a song that's about shaking your body back up on your feet again? That's the part I'm struggling with.

Get a Gym Membership

My daughter joined a gym yesterday. The idea is if you pay money to come and exercise, you might do it. They advertise it as a judge-free zone. I mean, I'm sure if they're promising not to judge when I walk through the doors, they'll keep their word as the business owners. But what about the other sixty people who are in there using the equipment? Did they sign something that said they wouldn't laugh as they are benching 250 while I'm working for the entire fourteen minutes to get the treadmill adjusted to sloth speed?

Order a Small Exerciser for $19.99 from a TV Ad

These come in bright colors and the smiling models on TV have never had so much fun in their lives. With Super Duper Arm Spin or Ab Blaster 2000, you can have the body you've always dreamed of. It looks like more fun than a carnival ride with half the queasiness, and you can hardly get to your phone fast enough, and get it shipped right to your door. Which is pretty much where it stays once you put it between your legs, try to squeeze it together, and end up with bruised thighs and a broken coffee table.

Just Use Household Items as Exercise Tools

The physical therapist taught us to do this with Dad. We used the kitchen sink as a pull-up bar, and cans of soups for weights. I mean, face it, I always questioned the intelligence of using something called a dumbbell. Soup just makes more sense.

Whatever method you land on, just make sure you're as busy as a bee, working like a horse, and sweating like a pig. Because when the fourteen minutes are up, and you find out you're still in the same dress size, you're going to be mad as a hornet!

Train Your Dragon for HUMILITY

Realize It Never Was About Me

Key Scriptures
Proverbs 16:18; Luke 14:11; 18:4; Philippians 2:8;
1 Peter 5:5; 2 Corinthians 9:15

Our collie had a problem with humility. She had an ongoing one-up contest with the beagle next door. Those were the days before we knew leftovers were bad for your pet, so each day she got up asking, "What's for dinner?"

Now the answer is the same for every dog. "You know those dried-up liver balls you've had for the last 8429 nights? Guess what?" But not back then. So Lassie would size up the menu when her dish was set down at night, and before she would take a bite, she would run and compare her winnings with the beagle's.

I couldn't understand a word of their conversation of course. But I think it went something like:

"Oh yeah? Well, I've got cornbread *and* meatloaf. Top that."

"Fettucine alfredo."

"Oh, quit it with the arrogant accent. Probably came from the freezer aisle. Anyway, I got butter beans on the side."

"Yeah, with fake butter I bet."

They went on like this for a couple of minutes before pride gave way to hunger and they returned to their bowls of scraps.

But there's something that those who don't read their Bible—like Lassie—did not know that the rest of us should. "Pride goes before destruction, and a haughty spirit before a fall" (Proverbs 16:18).

One night Lassie was particularly braggadocious because she had fried chicken on her plate. But it was in the spring, and those who knew my father at all knew that every spring, Daddy dug a ditch. There was always a surface reason—he had to replace a portion of a pipe; he had to allow the washing machine to drain; he had an underground smuggling operation—I don't know, but as sure as the grass began to grow lush and green and the birds began to migrate back home, Daddy had a strong hankering to pick up a shovel and ruin whatever spring appeal our yard was beginning to muster.

So as Lassie began to wind things up in her bragging session with the beagle and head back for her bowl, she decided to take a slight detour for a finale. She saw the three-foot-high pile of dirt on her side of the ditch but didn't know what was beyond it. It was an unavoidable temptation to give herself a running start and gracefully bound over the pile of dirt on her way to supper as the beagle stared on. I know she was repeating in her head, "I hope I can clear it." She did, with her sable coat blowing in the breeze. But you know what's next.

She misjudged the landing. And she toppled like a fourth-down sacked quarterback in slo-mo. The dog who seconds ago had imagined herself to be a majestic gymnast of Olympic proportions now stood in utter humiliation, when she could stand at all. She tucked her tail between her legs, an expression of shame came over her face, and she wasn't making eye contact with any of us. It was a good little while before she found the determination to pull herself out when no one was looking. Had it not been for fried chicken calling her name, she might be there to this day.

If she had ever been to Bible class, another verse would have come to mind. "For everyone who exalts himself will be humbled, and he who humbles himself will be exalted" (Luke 14:11).

Gentle and Lowly

There is a dragon or two that could learn from Lassie. Self-promotion is our first language, but humility is Christ's. At the heart of God is meekness and lowliness. "For I am gentle and lowly in heart" (Matthew 11:29).

Why else would the Son of God almighty be born in a barn instead of a palace and placed in a feeding trough instead of a royal crib of gold draped in the finest and rarest of linens? We plan our nurseries from the time the litmus paper shows up positive (or before), we have church friends around us who bring on the accessories with a side of punch and cucumbers, and we register for just what we want in the color we want and the embroidery font we want. And yet here was Emanuel, God with us, in more humble surroundings than we could have drawn up. But God's drawings know no limits. Somehow I see Mary looking at it all and saying, "This is not what I registered for."

But God was here. On earth. "In the beginning was the Word, and the Word was with God, and the Word was God. He was in the beginning with God. All things were made through him, and without him was not any thing made that was made" (John 1:1–3). There is no higher rung. Who would this supreme dignity and deity rub elbows with? Surely it would be with the most prominent and the most affluent. But who is it that really made the cut?

So His fame spread throughout all Syria, and they brought him all the sick, those afflicted with various diseases and pains, those oppressed by demons, those having seizures, and paralytics, and he healed them (Matthew 4:24).

These are usually not the first people on the guest list for the debutant.

And what about His ride? If there had been a Ferrari or Bugatti in that era, it would not have been suitable for such a King of kings. Surely He would have had the most highly bred, trained, and groomed camel adorned in the most ornate of necklaces, beads, pendants, and tassels. It would not be on our radar to think of the lowly ride Jesus had as He entered Jerusalem, but again, God's gentle and lowly heart can come up with things beyond our scope. And so the ride into Jerusalem was not only on a donkey, but on a colt that had never been ridden. I can picture that the animal was pretty awkward since it had no idea what was going on. If this wasn't bad enough, the vehicle was borrowed.

Ever had times so tough that you had to get from here to there in a borrowed vehicle? The late Eugene Hibbett let me borrow his Volkswagen, when I was a poor college student, to go to the next town. College professors don't make a heap either, and so I remember just guessing and praying it was in the right gear as the shift knob just kind of wobbled between the four speeds.

My son stood in line for freshmen registration at that same college some twenty-five years later, but he had a car. Sort of. It was nineteen years old, had been wrecked before he acquired it, and had been repaired with a front quarter panel that was a different color from the rest of it. He couldn't even afford that kind of car, but his uncle had given it to him. He had most of the blanks filled in on the form that the college required to get a parking pass, but he looked at me in despair and said, "Mom, it asks what color." Pause. "Should I just put multi-colored?"

We get what it is like to have a ride that doesn't make the latest cover of *Hot Rod* magazine. But a lot of prominent people don't get that. It just doesn't happen to the elite of society. And yet it was Jesus Christ's choice. He could have, on the spot, created a sports car of incredible magnitude that would have left all other cars in the dust and us with our jaws hanging open. But He chose the most humble and awkward to show the heart of the greatest King, and so His saddle becomes borrowed coats, and His red carpet was nothing but branches.

Behold, your king is coming to you; righteous and having salvation is he, humble and mounted on a donkey, on a colt, the foal of a donkey (Zechariah 9:9).

The Greatest

It's a stark contrast to our way of thinking and our way of speaking. Our dragons want to clarify which spoon is the best in the silverware drawer. And the same dragon waves it around for everyone to see, takes a selfie with it, and puts it on a T-shirt. The question in Matthew 18 was sure to come because it's who we are. We want to know who's the greatest. Who's the greatest quarterback of all time, who won the most Grammys, who's the richest person in the world? I'm writing this chapter near a ball park between games of round one of the national softball championship. We can't wait to see who's going to come out on top.

For thousands of years, we've been consumed with the greatest, so the question was bound to come up. The disciples wanted to know who was the greatest in the kingdom. *Give us your best cabinet member,* they basically said, each one probably hoping deep down that they would be nominated. But Jesus took a little child and set him in the midst of them. Reckon he was dirty? Reckon he fell a little short of the criteria they were accustomed to when selecting a leader? I'm pretty sure he shuffled around and couldn't stay still as he cut his eyes around the circle there. He didn't know what was going on because no one had ever singled him out before, and he was neither hoping for it nor expecting it. He was humble. And Jesus said,

Whoever humbles himself like this child is the greatest in the kingdom of heaven (Matthew 18:4).

What Did Jesus Choose?

Jesus consistently chose the lowliest of surroundings, the lowliest of rank, and the most disdained of men to drive home the greatest of teachings: a hometown of Nazareth, an inner circle of fishermen and tax collectors, lunch dates with the unpopular, and no bed at bedtime. All of these are brought out in scripture. He could have had better. But He chose humility.

He chose it until the earthly end. We have no choice about our death, but sometimes we talk about what we would choose if we could. Quick and easy. Comfortable. Surrounded by love and support. There was one who could choose, and here's what He chose.

> And being found in human form, he humbled himself by becoming obedient to the point of death, even death on a cross (Philippians 2:8).

It was neither quick nor easy. There was no comfort for six long hours of agony following many hours of torture. The environment was hostile as the mobs chanted for His crucifixion, and He was spat on and slapped. It was a death reserved for the most despicable and rejected of society. And yet absorb this if you can—He chose it for no other reason than love for me. The Hebrews writer confirms the reason:

> Looking to Jesus, the founder and perfecter of our faith, who for the joy that was set before him endured the cross, despising the shame, and is seated at the right hand of the throne of God (Hebrews 12:2).

Competing Tongues

It is sobering to think that God on high subjected Himself to these things on earth, but what does it have to do with my dragon? The tongue is the drainpipe for the heart. "But what comes out of the mouth proceeds from the heart, and this defiles a person" (Matthew 15:18).

If Jesus is gentle and lowly in heart, let's model our hearts after that one, and let's train our dragons to follow. A tongue that boasts and brags and competes with the dog next door doesn't stem from a humble heart. Why is it a temptation to convince others of our worth, of our talents, or of our deeds? Probably because Satan tempts us with anything that can narrow our influence and distract from a focus on God's greatness. A boasting dragon is so busy trying to steal the curtain call that she misses the beauty in others, and she fails to give glory to the great I AM. Consider Mrs. Da.

Everyone knows Lottie. She's introduced herself to everyone, and she'll also be glad to let you know how much she gave to the building fund, how long she's been a member, and that the sixth pew is hers.

Lottie is the youngest of the Da sisters—the prettiest, smartest, and richest of course. We all know that Lottie volunteers for the benevolence closet, that she arranged the flowers in front of the baptistery, and that she paid for the fabric for the bulletin board. The reason that we know is that Lottie has told us all. Countless times. Sometimes she says, "You do know whose idea it was to put hand sanitizer in the foyer, don't you?" And we all answer, "Lottie Da!"

Lottie Da never lacks for conversation. We try to talk about the weather or the flu or the half-price sale or anything at all, but Lottie says, "Enough about that, let's talk about me." We all say, "Well, all right then, Lottie Da!"

Lottie Da likes to be consulted before we do anything. She needs to know what color the VBS shirts will be before we order them, how many toothpicks will be at each table, and how many sheets of toilet paper will be on each roll. One wonders how it is that Jesus fed five thousand people without Lottie first approving a seafood menu and questioning the carbs in the five loaves.

Lottie Da is everywhere. She is the first to volunteer for every pretty job. Her talents are coveted, and every time she holds up one of her masterpieces for everyone to see, everyone says, "Well, Lottie Da!"

That is, until someone is needed to sit up with our beloved Gracie. It would require changing the bedpan and dressing the infection, but everyone was more

If Jesus is gentle and lowly in heart, let's model our heart after that one.

than willing to do that for someone as special as Gracie. Everyone, I guess, except Lottie Da. Where *did* that woman go? She was here a minute ago, but that was just before we started scraping the mold out of the refrigerator. Oh, I think someone sent Lottie Da to get a mop when that middle Rogers kid threw up.

Come to think of it, no one ever saw Lottie Da again.

How to Have a Humble Dragon

Sometimes our dragons try to outdo each other in outward appearances. Peter gives the formula for curing egotistic dragons:

> Likewise, you who are younger, be subject to the elders. Clothe yourselves, all of you, with humility toward one another, for "God opposes the proud but gives grace to the humble" (1 Peter 5:5).

So how do we bench pride and suit up in humility?

- *Avoid the temptation to correct or put down the other dragons in the lair.* I love autocorrect on my phone. It causes me to send and receive funny texts like, "I will meet you at Steam and Shame"; "Is thy heart right with 28th goat?"; and "Is it okay to pour the sugar in the dugout?" But I don't care at all for walking, breathing autocorrect dragons. If my soul is in jeopardy, yeah! Correct me! Let's turn this ship around before it hits a spiritual iceberg. But if this is about a line from a character in a rerun of *Kung Fu*, leave it. If you have to start your sentence with *technically*, this is too technical. The humble dragon does not wait eagerly for an error so he can better his value at the expense of someone else's. Even if you're right all the time, here's a tip for you—no one wants to know.

- *Turn self-admiration around and reflect it on others.* In my opinion, we have become so hung up on the two words *as yourself* in Matthew 22:39 that we forget that the whole idea of the verse is to love someone else! We forget there is a much clearer treatise on self-esteem, if that's what we're looking for:

> For by the grace given to me I say to everyone among you not to think of himself more highly than he ought to think, but to think with sober judgment, each according to the measure of faith that God has assigned (Romans 12:3).

Continue from Romans 12:3 through verse 13 and you'll see that striking the right balance of self-evaluation has much to do with re-focusing on both the needs and the strengths of others.

The morning shows and pop psychologists may tell us to pat ourselves on the backs, but dragons have spiky backs and we end up with nothing but raw paws. When our friends begin to congratulate us and build us up, let's redirect and turn that light around. "You made my morning with your kind words. God gave you the gift of encouragement."

Specifically let people know how they have helped you along your journey. They will never know unless your dragon tells them. If you have achieved some milestone that you have worked hard for and prayed long about, remember those who got you there. First of all, it was our merciful Father. But within that, never forget the acknowl-edgements page. "I remember you told me that day after worship that I would get through this." "I remember you taught me when I was a little girl in Bible class, and you instilled in me a love for study." "I remember watching you when you came to worship and you had cancer, and your determination impacted me." It is in these treasures of memories of those who have carried you that your dragon shuts its mouth of boasting, and you know beyond doubt that all the accolades belong to someone else.

- *Most important, drown your pride in thankfulness.* Nothing is as despi-cable as ingratitude. My mother loved fried fish better than anyone I have ever known. One meal, we had a particularly large catch of it. My mother had finished off a small piece and was reaching for a second when the evening ritual happened. Our outdoor cat jumped from the porch to the screen of the window where she belly danced for our dinner entertainment all the way to the top, and then drop-landed on the air conditioner which was like a VIP box seat for meal viewing. Who couldn't feel sorry for a cat licking her lips and putting on her sad eyes as she stared at the seafood feast?

My mother caved in to her theatrics, and as much as she loved fish, she stood up, took her plate to the back door and set it in front of the cat who could somehow make the return trip from the window unit to the porch in one leap and with much less fanfare. She was there staring at the prize before Mother got the plate all the way on the ground. But instead of swallowing it whole, she looked at it taking a trip around the plate. She sniffed it a few times as if she were trying to guess a perfume, and then she did the most despicable act of all. She licked it. She licked it! And then she walked away to—I don't know—sign autographs, I guess. How unthankful! To the woman who had cared for her and sacrificed what she loved best.

Train Dragons to Purr with Thanks

How despicable are we? God cares for us, sacrificed the one He loved best, and we walk away to sign autographs without even saying, "Thank You." The Bible warns so much against pride that I have really begun to second guess saying, "I'm proud of . . ." I know it is meant as an encouragement to others in our sphere of influence, to motivate them to even greater heights of service, so I'm not really getting on to you if you tell your kids or grandkids, "I'm proud of you." I'm just wondering if a better way to communicate the message is to say,

- "I'm thankful for you."

- "When I think of all you have done and been these last sixteen years, I am deeply thankful."

- "I saw you taking notes during the sermon, and I am so thankful for you."

- "You have the biggest heart, and I want you to know, I thank God for you."

I understand that it's a fine line and communicates a similar message of encouragement, but it shifts the focus where it belongs. And what child, what brother or sister in Christ, isn't nourished, sustained, motivated, and emotionally driven by knowing that he or she is a blessing celebrated with thanksgiving to God? And we have biblical precedent:

First, I thank my God through Jesus Christ for all of you, because your faith is proclaimed in all the world (Romans 1:8).

Train your dragon for thanksgiving. And have that dragon train all the little dragons for thanksgiving. The first thing to say when your children show you what the teacher gave them in class is, "Did you say thank you?" And if not, send them back to do it. I have a feeling that there are some Bible class teachers who say, "Where are the nine?" (Luke 17:17), and sometimes, "Where are the ten?" This leprosy-healing episode is a great lesson in saying thank you to one another. But it is so much more.

Jesus gave His life to cleanse us of the sin disease—the one disease that trumps all other diseases; the one that destroys our lives, many lives that our lives touch, and the one that reaches beyond the grave and destroys our eternity. Praise God, we can be healed. Jesus Christ paid the price for our sin on the cross, and it can be washed away forever. Yet, nine out of ten choose ingratitude over gratitude for healing.

Humility Requires Training

When I was a little girl, we each brought a Christmas present to school on the last day before Christmas break, and drew numbers to see who would get what. When my mother was a little girl, they drew names, and picked out a present specifically for the child whose name they drew. She told me about an occasion when a poor girl drew the name of a very rich little girl. When the poor girl got home that afternoon, her mother scolded her for participating in the game. They had no extra money; they could not buy a gift. The little girl went to her bedroom and cried and cried.

Her older brother heard her sobbing, and when he found out the reason, he went to his room and got a nickel he had earned. It was enough for a child to buy something back then. She was elated!

She went to the variety store holding her nickel tightly, and walked up and down the aisle like a cat waiting for an open door. She picked up cheap toys and turned them over in her hands until finally it was decided. She purchased something she had never owned—a full box of crayons, each with the paper still on and the points still sharp. She went home, wrapped it in newspaper, and couldn't sleep all night because of the excitement.

When the time came for the gift exchange, the rich little girl tore open the package, and said, "Crayons? Why would I want that?" and tossed them aside without as much as a thank you.

Heartbreaking, isn't it? Imagine the heart of God, now that He has given us His very best—from creation to the providential care He provides through all our days to the last bite of beans we put in our mouths, and then ultimately, the very best. "For God so loved the world, that he gave his only Son, that whoever believes in him should not perish but have eternal life" (John 3:16). If the thought of that doesn't train our dragons for humility, nothing will.

Thanks be to God for his inexpressible gift! (2 Corinthians 9:15).

TRAINING POINTS

1. I don't think we can find the words "I'm proud" in scriptures in a positive light. However, there are many times that other words are used to convey the thought of appreciation for another person or his or her deeds. Find some of these.

2. List six parallels between leprosy and sin.

3. I wonder what was going on in the now leprosy-free men that distracted them from saying thank you for such a monumental life-changing gift. Theorize on what some of these things could have been based on your knowledge of what distracts us from thanking God today.

4. Three ways were suggested to veer our dragons away from self-promotion. One was to avoid the temptation to one-up others by correcting them. The second was to redirect any praise of self so that it might encourage others instead, and the third was to replace pride with thankfulness. Of these three, which do you think we miss the mark on the most. How and why?

5. The summation of this study leads us to the conclusion that we train the dragon first by training the heart. If there is a sister in Christ that Satan tempts you to compete with in some way—if you have thoughts kin to Lassie's about my supper's better than yours—pray for that person every single day this week. Pray that her efforts will be successful, that God will bless her, and that she will have a great influence in the kingdom.

6. How can we humble ourselves like the little child Jesus refers to in Matthew 18:4? Make a list of great characteristics children have that adults have let go of. Listen to children this week, and make notes as to which of their sayings reflect a humble curiosity or innocence not yet ruined by pride. Share a favorite quote from a child you know. Not all of them will reflect humility because of the world they are learning from, but pick one that does.

7. Ask yourself, "How have I tossed my box of crayons aside today?" What blessing today, or in recent days, did you forget to say thank you for, and possibly even complained about instead?

8. Are the children you know assigned to bring Christmas gifts on the last day before Christmas break? Did your classes do that when you were in school? How has the tradition changed and why?

9. Recall a time when you had a gift for someone that you were beside yourself about giving, and you could hardly wait to see the expression on their face when they opened it. Was it hard to acquire the gift? How and where did you get it? How does this help us understand, on some level, the emotion of God attached to "His inexpressible gift"?

10. How do we know where the line is between correcting someone and letting it go? What are some criteria we can think quickly about to know whether our dragons should open their mouths or not?

11. In 1 Peter 5:5, there are quotation marks around part of this verse in our translations. What other New Testament writer uses the same quotation, and where? There is also an Old Testament proverb that is similar. Where is it, and what does it say?

THE TAIL END

And Speaking of the Sacked Quarterback . . .

February always brings with it a nostalgic look back at some presidential greats as well as the legacy of black history. Valentine's Day will bring romantic sweetness, but let us never forget what it's all about—loaded nachos and buffalo wings!

The first Sunday night of each February, we hold a house party. It's called Second Half at the Sparks. We're worshiping and enjoying fellowship with the rest of the Christians just like every Sunday during the first half. But after "the last amen," there's a mass exodus to the parking lot and north to our subdivision.

We're not so experienced in football, but we've learned a few strategies through the years. First is what we do about the tight end. This is the end of the kitchen in which the refrigerator door opens directly across from where the oven door opens, and for some reason, everyone who walks in the front door proceeds to that point, and then stops. It looks like I-24 in Atlanta at 5:01 on bring-an-extra-car-to-work day. There must be a magnetic field here that prevents anyone from deciding to meander anywhere else in the house. My husband serves as offensive coach for the party, and he handles it beautifully by yelling, "Everyone get out of the kitchen!" I don't think he read this in *Tips for Entertaining Dinner Guests Elegantly*, but it works nonetheless, particularly the third time.

Next, we realize we have too many running backs on the gridiron. We're good when the commercials are on and have actually thought of renaming the party *Suddenly-Congregate-at-the-Screen-When-a-Commercial-Comes-On Night*, but as soon as the game resumes, all the running back to the table occurs. We had enough plates to support the Styrofoam industry through 2030, and still ran out. Once, we huddled for a prayer before the first invasion to the table, and as soon as "Amen" was said, I opened the oven door to get pigs in blankets out, and I couldn't even usher them to the table before all the piggies' blankets were pulled back and they were out of bed and halfway down the digestive track.

Finally, all the running backs produce several full backs, which is about the time people just begin to plop wherever gravity pulls them. They no longer sit on the edge of their seats or bounce up for interceptions. They just slowly talk about the Super Bowl of '88, the referee's hair, and Alka-Seltzer.

Research shows that in the last two minutes of the game, also known as the last thirty-seven minutes of the game, the crowd musters their energy again and actually pays attention. At this point, the strategy is to bite off all your nails as time-outs are called and replays are shown and arguments erupt in which it seems every man in the room missed his calling as a national sports commentator. Researchers further estimate that ninety percent of these people completely forget that they have any kids. That's about the time I realize I better check the red zone. This is the part of the field covered with red Kool-Aid, ketchup, and Flamin' Hot Cheetos crumbs, and formerly known as the play room. Recovery is slow, lasting into the World Series for us, so I send all the kids back downstairs before any more damage is done.

That's not a good plan either. One year, seven-year-old James bounced back downstairs, looked at the milkshake maker, and said, "What's that thing?"

"It's a milkshake maker," I whispered, "and if you're really good, I'll make you one a little later."

"FREE MILKSHAKES FOR EVERYONE!!!" James yelled to the entire guest list. I was scooping ice cream until Easter.

Yeah, we definitely have a few crazy moments, but it adds to the memory-making of family-and-friends-together time. And what would an event like this be without time-honored traditions? One such tradition we observe year after year is the post-game who's-car-is-stuck-in-the-ditch-this-time gala. This is complete with spinning tires, muddy dry-clean-only coats, and eventually a chain and slightly stretched bumper.

This February, I'll make a few hand-cut valentines, display my husband's presidential statue collection, have the kids do a little research on black heritage, but when it comes to Super Bowl Sunday, I think I may save a step, skip the party, and go straight to completely destroying the property.

(Originally printed in *Christian Woman* magazine, J/F 2015)

WORKS CITED

Barry, Dave. *The Seattle Times*, January 13, 1992.

CNN, Cable News Network, "Larry King Live," 11 March 2003, transcripts.cnn.com.

Fulwiler, Michael. "Announcement: The Research," *The Gottman Institute*, 11 February 2013. The Gottman Relationship Blog.

Gervais, Rick and Rob Steer. *Flanimals Pop-Up* (Somerville, Mass.: Candlewick Press, 2010).

Hodgson, Godfrey. *A Great and Godly Adventure; The Pilgrims and the Myth of the First Thanksgiving* (New York: Public Affairs, 2006), p. 167.

Seuss, Dr. *The Cat in the Hat* (New York: Random House, 1985), p. 18.

Starnes, Todd. "Teacher Tells Student He Can't Read the Bible in Classroom." *Fox News*, Fox News Network, 5 May 2014.

Starnes, Todd. "School Sends Sheriff to Order Child to Stop Sharing Bible Verses." *Fox News*, Fox News Network, 3 June 2016.

"Thanksgiving." https://en.wikipedia.org/wiki/Thanksgiving.

CPSIA information can be obtained
at www.ICGtesting.com
Printed in the USA
LVHW050908180119
604353LV00002B/2